# Threading Time

Tricia Cake

# Threading Time
## A memoir

In memory of Dr Fred Bell

Thank you to all my family and children for their love, and to my husband Graeme for his love and support over the years. To my brother John, the best brother ever, thank you.

To my friend Joy Want, who kept encouraging me to finish the book. To Sue Cattell, who read my book and who walked part of my journey with me, thank you. And Dr Solveig Hamilton, sadly now deceased, who read my book and encouraged me.

But most of all, my heartfelt thanks go to my son Tim for his many hours of editing, his expertise, endless patience and keen sense of humour. I enjoyed the many hours we spent laughing and sharing memories.

## Acknowledgements

While many books have influenced the writing of *Threading Time*, I would like to make particular mention of three: Joan Chittister's *Scarred by Struggle, Transformed by Hope*; Dorothy Rowe's *Beyond Fear*; and David A. Karp's *Speaking of Sadness*. Each of them in their own way provided a guide and an inspiration for *Threading Time*.

*Threading Time: A memoir*
ISBN 978 1 76041 267 8
Copyright © Tricia Cake 2016

First published 2016 by
**GINNINDERRA PRESS**
PO Box 3461 Port Adelaide 5015
www.ginninderrapress.com.au

# Contents

Part One                            9

Part Two                           55

Part Three                        101

I sought the Lord, and he heard me, and
delivered me from all my fears.
Psalm 34

This above all: to thine own self be true,
And it must follow, as the night the day,
Thou canst not then be false to any man.
Shakespeare, *Hamlet*

Understanding is the reward of faith.
Therefore, seek not to understand that you may believe
but believe that you may understand.
Saint Augustine

# Part One

# 1

It was in 1960 that I passed my leaving certificate and gained a scholarship to Sydney University. I was seventeen. To my surprise, I had obtained a good pass in my exams. School was behind me and I was excited about the future. A new life beckoned. The sun shone brightly over Sydney and the world was at my feet. Or should have been.

This was the beginning of the next phase of my life. I was enrolled in the Faculty of Arts to study Latin, French, Ancient History and Psychology, with the aim of qualifying to teach Latin in high schools. As part of a teachers' college scholarship, I was to receive an allowance of four pounds a week.

With my newly found independence and the future looking good, I should have been happy. But for me, university life was overwhelming, unfamiliar in all its ways, and I struggled, feeling unable to adjust. I was lost among the hundreds of students who had their friends, their books and their lives, chattering in small groups, eating lunch together and laughing happily. I felt quite alone.

I walked the grounds of Sydney University between my lectures. The grounds were well-established and pleasant. There were large grassed areas with seats, and trees provided a canopy over them. The birds in the trees and nature itself afforded a sense of peace as I tried to find a way of coping in this new environment, to make friends and enjoy university life.

Every morning when I woke up, I would get dressed and eat breakfast, then I would walk up McPherson Street – quite a steep hill – until I reached Military Road. It was a good walk, ten or fifteen minutes, and from there I caught a bus into the city. This usually took forty-five minutes, as the traffic crossing Sydney Harbour Bridge was very heavy in peak hour. On reaching the city, I would catch another bus from George Street; this bus went along Parramatta Road to Sydney University. Crossing the road, I walked up the old stone steps. They were big wide steps, perhaps to allow for the hundreds of students who climbed them every day. I imagined the students of past generations who had already placed their footprints on these steps and I thought about their lives.

One day, I saw my Latin professor walking down these steps to catch his bus; he was carrying the biggest packet of cornflakes I have ever seen. I laughed.

I attended lectures and worked hard each evening to do the required readings for the following day. I handed in all my assignments, still doubting my ability but passing my exams nevertheless. But I was merely going through the motions. Lonely, I stumbled on from one day to the next. On two afternoons each week I worked at Coles, weighing up confectionery, which I quite enjoyed. I was earning money, and was able to save. I worked there for most of the year, and during the long Christmas break I worked full-time at Farmers, which is now called Myer.

After passing my first year of university, I decided I didn't want to continue there for another two years. I transferred to Sydney Teachers' College to complete one more year of what was then called an ex-university course. This would enable me to teach Latin and English in high schools, but only from first to third year. I was happier at teachers' college, the pressure was less; it was more like school in fact. I was still alone, but the environment was more friendly.

**The Boy With His Turtle**

The bird soars to the sky on wings that are free
No captive to another's bonds.
A little boy approaches and proudly displays a turtle in his bucket
His face alive with excitement and wonder
He goes on to discover his world
The trees stand tall and stately
Portraying a sense of peace –
The same yesterday, today and forever
As surely the warmth of the sun beats down over all.

Warm and loving, it gradually penetrates further
And begins to thaw the cold aching depths,
A core untouched except by God
Within it and within each one of us lies the answer to the wonders and mysteries of our universe.
Dare we search for the key to unlock this truth?

Perhaps it belongs only to the poets and mystics of our time
Who bear for us the anxieties and insecurities of an age yet to come.
To live with this truth is painful,
Separated from the realities of life yet living therein.

He yearns to share the treasures he has uncovered.
Alone, misunderstood; yet he remains
The keeper of the key
A lone pilgrim in an undiscovered land
A premature experience of the future of mankind...
To communicate it... A lost hope.
The sun remains,
The warmth of love God promised.
Unfailing, never ending it bridges the gap
And links aloneness to the reality of life.

The boy returns, his turtle is now back in the stream.
He exchanges a few words,
A spontaneous expression of joy
Two paths cross...an experience of unity.
His words echo in the distance,
'I'll see you tomorrow.'

I arrived at the psychologist's door. His name was Wilfred Jarvis. Once a week I went to see him and he would ask me whether I had eaten a bowl of cereal for breakfast. At that stage I was not eating very well and was losing weight. I was eighteen, and had just started at Sydney Teachers' College. As I said, it was more familiar to me than university life, but nevertheless I was not coping very well. I was still finding life very difficult. I was attending lectures, doing the required work and completing assignments, but still struggling to keep up. I felt estranged from life – it was as if I were in a different world. Many times I was at the office of the Dean of Women asking for help to survive in this environment. Work was piling up. I felt unable to cope, swimming in deep waters unable to keep afloat.

This continued for a year. I did my work, and with the help of the psychologist and the Dean of Women I managed to pass my exams, although I still lacked confidence in my ability. I completed the obligatory practice teaching, but the experience filled me with anxiety. Still, I ate breakfast every morning and somehow or other I pulled through. Life at home went on as usual.

It was now towards the end of 1962 and the following weeks would be spent waiting for a letter in the mail. This was sent to each student advising them of the school to which they had been appointed for the following year. Usually teachers in their first year out were sent to the country.

And so it was that I was sent to Kiama, a beautiful town on the south coast of New South Wales, past Wollongong, an hour or two's drive south of Sydney. It was an idyllic seaside country town. My grandmother offered to come with me once she knew that I had been posted there. She had always loved Kiama. We would share a place together. My grandfather had died a few years earlier and she was lonely. And so we rented a little flat and she taught me to cook. I loved being with her. She was a wonderful person and was always there for me. I was her only granddaughter out of nine grandchildren, and she often told me how special I was.

At the school, I was teaching English and Latin. English to the first, second and third years and Latin to all years right through to fifth year. So, at nineteen, I was teaching students just two years younger than myself. This was necessary as it was a small country school. They were great young people. It was exciting. The first year students were my favourites. I took down a pile of books with me from home and created a small class library for them. The memories of that time are otherwise very hazy as I was only there for a short time, possibly only three months, and I was not very well. I managed to teach the English classes I had, but what I really enjoyed was teaching Latin.

The staff there were always very supportive. In spite of that, I found teaching quite difficult. It was very scary. It seems strange to me now, looking back, that every weekend I would get into my little cream-coloured car, a Morris Minor, and rush home – back to Sydney. My grandmother, whom I loved so much, was left there on her own. I would just take off at 3.30 on a Friday afternoon for the two-hour journey, speeding most of the way, and quite unconcerned about the safety of my passengers. Was it just to see my mother?

It was almost like a dream: floating in and out of classrooms, meals with my grandmother and the frenetic trip home at weekends.

Time passed, and the staff at the school were very concerned, especially the headmaster. I felt his watchful eye on me. Eventually I was unable to hold it all together, and one day it unravelled, tumbling out in big bursts and I ran out – out of the classroom, into my car – and I drove off. Usually in my car I felt safe, protected. But I felt overwhelmed and out of control.

All at once I found myself at the Blowhole, a well-known attraction overlooking the ocean in Kiama. I stood there, gazing over the edge. It was a long, long way down. My heart was racing; I felt it might break through my chest, its sound was so loud in my ears. Fear took hold of me, my body skipping to fast-forward, desperately searching for an answer. But there wasn't one.

**Fear**

The reeds as they rustle with the wind,
Gently blend with the sun as they sway,
The gentleness of understanding,
And the peace and love it brings.
Can it break the frightening clasp of claws
That bind with fetters of fear?

To escape would be a relief from pain,
But is this life?
The swans glide along so peaceful, serene,
A message of hope they impart,
What is life but moments of fear and pain?
For without them the beauty of love is but a dream.

The love of God surely knows this suffering,
The fear that makes the way so frightening,
And so He shows his love…
In the gentleness of one who has suffered
And shared our pain.

    He found me there, standing on the edge, unable to move. It was all very frightening. The headmaster had come to look for me. At once I felt him beside me. How long I had been there I don't remember. He gently guided me from the edge of the Blowhole, his arm around me. I don't have any memory of what happened after that.

# Two

Growing up in the fifties in Sydney was an era like no other – privileged when you compare it with the lives of many of us. Children led a carefree life and had the freedom to roam as long as they were home when the street lights came on. It was the late forties and fifties when I grew up, and sixties really. How long does it take you to grow up? I played at the park and sat on the swings, talking to the children who were there.

There was a colour and a shape to my life. I played all my 45-rpm records on my record player and absorbed the rhythms and sounds of the times. There was a culture as always, a way ahead, a marked path. There were expectations. To work was important. The Protestant ethic was in full swing. You needed to be occupied, no messing around, no dreaming, no wasting time reading; you were expected to keep busy, at least in my house you were.

In Sydney at the time, Mosman was an affluent suburb and has remained so over the years. It is situated on the north side, close to Balmoral beach and Manly. My parents were fortunate to have bought in Mosman in 1940, with some financial assistance from relatives. It was a perfect place for a child to grow up. Sydney was established and thriving, and in the sixties it seemed like there was full employment. You had a choice of jobs. If you were unhappy in your job, you could get another one the next day.

My brother and I grew up five houses from the end of Awaba Street. McPherson Street was the boundary between Mosman and Cremorne. There was a big difference between an address in Mosman and one in Cremorne. Your postcode, according to my mother, was very important. Instead of catching the ferry from Cremorne Wharf, which was closer, she would drive to Mosman Wharf.

For the first twenty or so years of my life, when people would ask where I lived, I would tell them that I lived in Mosman. They would then look at me with 'that look'. Did I, perchance, think myself a cut above everyone else because I lived in Mosman? For the next forty years, I lived in another state. When I bought a house there, I was quite unaware of 'the best suburbs to live in'. Sometimes when I told people where I lived the response was something like the reverse.

Mosman was a 'good' middle-class suburb, even in the fifties, though there were plenty of ordinary people living there. It is an older suburb of Sydney, close to the city, and close to the water. Today very few people are able to afford to buy a house in Mosman. But there I grew up and there I lived until I was twenty-three. For most of the time, I loved it there.

Every Sunday morning, with an apple in each hand, I walked out the front door. Munching on my apple, I ran down the uneven front steps from our house to the street below. Huge rocks that were thickly covered with vines enclosed the steps. There was a hand-sized hole in the rock at the bottom of the steps, a secret place to store my treasures. I would walk down the steps, past the letterbox, turn and walk down some more steps. My footprints in turn marked each step. They mingled with those of others, family members and visitors who sometimes came to our front door. I went up and down these steps so many times and knew each one, its roughness, its uneven parts, the slippery ones. A certain way, a certain pattern.

'Could you run down the front steps for Mummy and pick up the paper?' my mother would ask. Or, 'Would you hop down the steps to the letterbox for Mummy. She's expecting a letter?'

As I child, I loved to do that. Poised precariously on the rocks at the top of the steps was the letterbox, well rusted from the frequent heavy rain in those days.

'Oh look, someone's coming up the front steps. I wonder who it is. Go and let them in, will you?' she would ask. And there was just enough time for her to put on some lipstick before they emerged at the top of the steps.

Steps are significant in my world. They always lead somewhere, reminding me of life's surprises. Steps took me to some places and enabled me to escape from others. I walked up the old well-worn steps to university and teachers' college, and up and down the steps within the many hospitals in which I worked. Comings and goings make up the fabric of one's life, really, weaving a pattern threaded with hope. Sorrow permeated those pathways, but always reminded me of the privilege of life.

I would walk, half run, down McPherson Street to my friend's house, passing the house of the two Bowring ladies, who had a garden full of beautiful flowers. My mother bought a bunch of flowers from the sisters, Glad and Lil, at three shillings a bunch – or was it three bunches? My mother loved to have fresh flowers in the house. I went to collect them for her every Saturday morning. They were quiet old ladies but significant figures in my life. I wondered what their lives were like as I waited in the kitchen for Glad to wrap up the flowers she had picked that morning. It was peaceful there.

On Sunday mornings, Dad went to church. When I was young, he took me and my brother with him, and we went to Sunday school. But as I got older, I didn't want to go any more. My mother stayed home and cooked the Sunday baked dinner; she never went to church. Sundays were one of the times when an argument between my parents would often erupt, usually as Dad was trying to get ready. I hated arguments, especially when they were loud and violent. So I had to get out. Every Sunday morning, I went to my friend Helen's house.

When I knocked on the door, her mother would answer in her nightgown, whatever the time of day it was, and say, 'Oh, it's early, Trisha. We're all still in bed. All right, come in. Helen's in her bedroom.'

I wanted to get out of my house, to see other people, other houses within which I imagined there was a different life. I knew all the houses along the way, having walked many paths through the suburb and its surrounds. I wondered who lived in them and whether their lives were happy.

I always tried to please my mother. When she left on Saturday mornings to go shopping in the city, I would start the vacuum cleaner and hoover the dining room and the lounge room, tidying and dusting as I went. Next I would go into the kitchen to clean and wash the floors, and then out on to the back veranda to sweep and mop. I did this so that when my mother came home she would not have to do any housework. I was pleased.

On Saturday afternoons, my mother ironed a full basket of clothes. Some of them were starched. She whistled while she worked. She was full of fun and had a great sense of humour. She used to chase my brother and me around the house, laughing and joking with us. They were fun times. But they were not to last, for life is not like that. The refrain on the turntable of my mother's radiogram played:

> Forever and ever
> My heart will be true
> Sweetheart forever
> I'll cherish you
>
> We both made a promise
> That we'd never part
> Let's seal it with a kiss
> Forever mine sweetheart
>
> Let bygones be bygones forever
> We'll fall in love once again
> So let's tell the world of our new love divine
> Forever and ever
> You'll be mine

My mother loved this record. She played it over and over. It seemed to me a cruel reminder of what was not to be. An illusion of a happy life, full of love and contentment. And as I looked around, because look around I did, I became aware of the lives of others, the ones that in my estimation were happy ones, and those similar to mine, which were not. I began to gather the facts about a happy life and continued to wonder what it was.

Visitors to our house were best not to carry happiness with them; if they did, they must remember to collect it when leaving, as happiness could not survive there.

Nicholas Christakis, a medical sociologist at Harvard medical school, studied the subject of happiness for many years. He found that 'a person's happiness was dependent to a greater or lesser degree on the happiness of their friend's friend, and their friend's friend's friend. An individual's chance at happiness increases the better they are connected…directly and vicariously to happy people.' For many years to come, I would ask whoever I was with of couples I would see, 'Is that a happy couple?' My goal was to find out, so I listened, I observed and I questioned.

When it was time to think of schools, my mother did not favour the closest school, which was about ten minutes' walk from home. She did not approve of the types of children who went there. At the age of five, I started at Killarney, a privately run infants' school in Mosman. I didn't like it. I cried every day and kept trying to run away. Sometimes I succeeded. It was quite a long way, and there was a busy road to cross before I was safely home. My feeling of elation was short lived, though. To my great disappointment, my mother was not at all pleased to see me. She took me straight back to school.

After a while, I became more devious in my escape attempts. I would ask to go to the toilet, and then quickly and quietly creep along the path up to the big heavy gate. I was only just able to open it, taking care that it did not squeak, and then I walked down the busy road until I got to the lane leading to Awaba Street, then I would run as fast as I could.

After the third occasion of returning me to school, my mother appeared very embarrassed. She decided to go to the local shop, where she bought ice creams for all of the children – except me. I felt humiliated in front of my classmates.

Schooldays were not the happiest days of my life, or so I have always believed. Images go through my mind quickly: I can see my old school playground and Miss Laver and Mrs Hall, my teachers, are there in front of me, and I feel the fear once again. I try to grab hold of the words so I can put them down on paper. It takes me back to the past.

Recently, on a trip to Sydney, I went back to Killarney. It's still there, and is probably heritage-listed by now. I noticed then that it was quite a long way from my childhood home – maybe twenty-five minutes' walk.

My mind flipped back and I was there again. I stood, transfixed, my gaze on the wooden gate overlaid with a sheet of metal, a hole cut in the side through which to slip the catch. My arms hung long and leaden by my side, fear rising within me as I gathered the courage to ease open the gate. I followed the cement path, now overgrown with grass and heavy moss. It led to the schoolroom. To the right, the playground was still there: a few trees around a cement area with the little wooden benches still stapled to the concrete. The smell of tomato sandwiches warmed by the morning sun wafted back to me on the breeze, placing me firmly back there once more. This was more than fifty years later.

From Killarney, which was the equivalent of infants' school, I was sent to a private school in Cremorne: SCEGGS, or Sydney Church of England Girls' Grammar School, Redlands. I knew no one. Most of the children from Killarney who I knew had gone on to Mosman Primary School. I would play alone behind the demountable buildings, collecting broken pieces of glass which I would line up and make patterns with, watching as the sun caught the edges of the glass, making pretty colours. I did not fit in. I rarely interacted with others. I didn't know what to say, not being able to identify with normal life.

I started off on the wrong foot as I was put in the class below the level I was at. The teachers disregarded the advice from my teachers at Killarney. There seemed to be some rivalry between schools regarding standards at the time. I knew all the work and was bored, so I talked to the children around me, distracting them from their work. Finally, the teachers realised they had made a mistake. 'At last,' I thought. Thus, after six months I was put up to the next class, but by then it was too late. I was not able to keep up with that class, by then having missed out on six months of lessons. I was betwixt and between. It took only a short time for the teachers to realise, and I was put back down once more.

Once again, I started talking to the other children and distracting them from their work. I had to write a hundred times, 'I must be good in school.' I was to write many more lines after that – and have kept some of them as a reminder. After receiving the punishment several times, I was given a detention. Then another, and another. After three detentions, I had a 'Black Saturday'. Yes, it is true, you had to go to school on Saturday, sit at a desk in the classroom and write lines, pages and pages of lines: 'I must be good in class' and 'I will never ever talk in class again.' I remember it well.

The headmistress was a strict disciplinarian and I didn't like her. My sense of justice was strong at an early age, and I just knew that the way she treated me was unfair. She was oblivious to me and my problems, and it was the last straw when I told her to 'shut up'. It was the last straw for me too, as I could bear it no longer. I was expelled or, to put it in the nicest terms, I was asked to leave. I started at Mosman Primary in fourth class but did not do well. In sixth class my teacher, Mrs Lupton, told me that I was 'stupid' and would probably end up at Mosman Home Science School, doing typing, dressmaking and cooking. As it turned out, I was among the girls going to Cremorne Girls' High School, where I did very well, doing subjects that I enjoyed. My teachers were excellent and very encouraging.

When I was about nine years old, my mother used to drive me to school. She would drop me there early in the morning so that she would be able to get to work on time. I used to wander the streets for half an hour before school. My mother did not know of course as she had left me there and would have expected me to have remained.

I found a beautiful place down near Clifton Gardens and Taronga Zoo. It was a patch of lovely lawn where tall trees had been growing for many years, protecting and watching over the place. The first time

I went there, I saw a lady wheeling a pram with her baby in it. She smiled at me and I was happy.

It became a safe place for me to be, a patch of beautiful green grass, where I could look up and see the blue, blue sky. The sun was shining; it was a peaceful place. I wished that I could be eighty years of age, and be able to stay there forever. It was warm and safe. Around me there were houses and I thought again about the people who lived in them and what their lives were like. I have revisited this place in my mind hundreds of times since, when things were difficult for me; it was my saving grace, my secret place where I felt safe. No one could get me, and no one could take it away from me.

**A Secret Place**

It's hard to fight the forces so great
To wish that it may or wish that it might
The grass is greener, the sun so warm
Could I just crawl here to stay alone?

For no harm can come where the warmth of the sun
Surrounds and protects whoever is there.
The sounds of the birds are clear and sweet,
I smell the grass that has just been mown
And the stones in the earth feel smooth and warm.

Through a cloud of mist and into the trees,
Across the bridge to clutch at the peace.
Out there in the sunshine once more to hide.
But lo calls the sound of truth.
Not here to stay but there I must go.

It's hard to hang on to the things around
Just a spark is needed to run it aground
For I'd rather be in a land that's free
Where the air is clear and the grass is fresh
The sounds so rich and clear.

The sound of music always calls me there
Away from the pressures that bear
Just a while to linger then away I will come
Some day to go there once more.

I went to my secret place before school and progressively strayed further down towards Taronga Zoo, looking at the houses and enjoying the sunshine. Sometimes I arrived late for school. It was a glorious freedom, a place and time to be myself, free from fear.

From an early age, the world was a wonder to me. Questions floated in my mind, knocking against each other but rarely producing answers. The kind of questions my mind asked were not the usual ones of a small child – How does the garden grow? What bird is that? What are those beautiful flowers called? Where is India? Those things did not interest me. It was enough for me that the world around and all that was in it was beautiful, and I immersed myself in its beauty on my walks. I enjoyed the warmth it created within me. Only then was I happy.

On the weekend, I walked miles around Mosman, Northbridge and Cammeray, exploring all the hidden pathways, private ones too. I imagined myself living in some of the houses. I was able to picture myself in them and become a part of them and them of me. I felt I belonged. In high school, I walked for hours after school. One day I walked as far as Manly. But my own world then, as now, I could not share with anyone. My life was not in step with others. I was different.

In 1956 I was twelve years old and just beginning high school. Cremorne Girls' High School was about forty minutes' walk from home. It was a good school in those days and I was fortunate to go there. My father left home early for work, and I liked to leave home with him, at seven-thirty, as I felt more at ease once I had left my home. It was a chance to spend time with him, just the two of us. I walked down the back lane, then down the big wide concrete steps. There was a railing down the middle and the steps were slightly curved. I'd walk across the road and up the big hill, which was McPherson Street, and from there I would see my father passing by in the bus. Wiping the tears from my eyes, I waved to him as his bus passed by. My heart was heavy my footsteps slowed. He waved to me. I smiled. He smiled back.

I was encouraged not to talk to my father. At least, it was better not to. My mother was the powerful one and it was important to stay on her side. It wasn't so easy, though, to listen to the constant criticisms she made of him. I especially disliked being caught in the car with her and being forced to listen to her tirades. More than once, I considered jumping out of the car, once even when we were crossing the harbour bridge. I always felt trapped.

Of all the houses on the way to school, certain fences and gates took my fancy and I looked for them every morning. People in their gardens coming out to get the paper or to leave for work would smile at me. That warmed my heart. Sometimes it was raining. Memorable to me was the weather forecast: 'rain for the weekend…set in'. And so it had. It did not stop. The weather remained dreary, wet, grey and miserable for the whole weekend. In order to get from our house to the back gate, even with an umbrella, you would have to run, and still you would be drenched. And it was not very far. On those days, I used to take my shoes off on the way to school and put them in my Globite case, putting them back on again when I arrived at school. The gutters streamed with water and there were puddles all the way.

The route to school provided a sense of security and familiarity. I walked that same route, varying it a little from time to time, for five years. It was familiar territory such that it became part of my world. I was at peace when I walked. As I was in no hurry to get home, I discovered different streets, little lanes and alleyways, and I knew the area like the back of my hand.

My mother was a very attractive woman, slim, with a good figure and looking years younger than she was. When she was eighty-six, she had to have a major operation and her surgeon described her as 'an eighty-six-year-old woman who looks sixty-five'. Much to my annoyance, from the time I was eleven years old people always asked whether we were sisters. My mother was thoughtful and kind to others. Our main complaint as children was that it seemed other people were always more important than we were.

She was concerned about the little boy down the street who had no shoes, and the man who worked at Mosman wharf who always made her a hot cup of coffee – she wanted to pay his dentist bill for him because 'he needs to have his teeth fixed'. And presents: my mother gave presents to everyone – expensive presents. It was a lovely trait, I later realised, but I was especially embarrassed when I had to give a present to our dentist, 'because he has been good to us', and to the conductor of the orchestra that I was in (well, he was just to be worshipped). We would drive to Lindfield to give it to him personally. And the doctor's receptionist of course deserved something nice because she had been so kind. Sometimes I feel sad, though, because now I find it hard to give presents and so I settle on just little ones, saying, 'It's the thought that counts.'

When I was seven years old, my parents bought a car, a Ford Prefect, number plate ND 765. They both seemed to be very excited and happy, for a while. It was also in 1950 that my mother started work, much to my father's disappointment and disapproval. Very few women worked in those days, where I lived, except those who were divorced, widowed or very poor. None of the above applied. No other mother I knew worked, except two who were in the above categories.

My mother was ahead of her time; she would have done well in the following generation. She worked every day in the city as a bookkeeper from nine a.m. till three p.m. She dropped us at school, early, saying, 'Quick, get out, I have to get to work.' I did not like her working, It made me different to most of the girls in class, whose mothers were home if they were sick. She did not allow us to be sick. It isn't fair, I thought. I only had a few days off school, ever. My mother's remedy for most ailments was 'Eat an orange and go out and sit out in the sun.' If you were really sick, you would be given two Bayer's aspirin and sent to school. The two days that I did have off from school were when I was sent home, at age sixteen, with German measles and told not to come back until the spots had gone.

School holidays were the times that I really felt the fact that I had a working mother. When we were younger, my brother and I were minded at a childcare centre, which I thought was awful. In those days, childcare facilities, usually in private homes, were not regulated and the care was far from good. I was quite young and my brother was only four. I was angry with the ladies who were supposedly caring for us as they treated my brother roughly and with little compassion, and I told them so. Every day of the school holidays I cried and begged my mother not to leave us there. When I heard the eighteen-month-old babies crying in their cots and no one attending to them, I was very upset. I tried to tell the caregivers that they were crying but they took no notice and brushed me away. They simply continued chatting among themselves while the babies became more distressed. I kept begging my mother to take us away. It took a while but eventually she realised and made other childcare arrangements.

My dad was thirteen years older than my mother. He came to Australia from Belfast in 1927 with all of his family, except for a married brother who stayed in Ireland. I loved my father. Since he died in 1998, I think of him often and of the things that he taught me. In times of uncertainty, I think, 'What would my dad have done?' Dad was thirty-nine, nearly forty, when I was born and forty-two when my brother was born. He used to tell us that older fathers produced more intelligent children. He was right about my brother. Dad wanted to migrate to Australia, make his fortune, and go back to Ireland and marry his cousin Nettie. But his mother had other ideas: 'If you go, we all go.' And they did. That is, except for Walter, my father's married elder brother, who remained in Ireland, promising to follow after them. He never did. When they arrived, they struggled to make ends meet, I was told; during the Depression my grandfather was unable to find work at first. My father, who was a qualified accountant, obtained work and became the main breadwinner. As it had been in Ireland, his mother depended on him financially.

My father's mother died from a heart attack a year after they arrived. She was unable to adjust and grieved for the son left behind. My Aunt Violet was working in Prouds, a jeweller's shop in the city, but the loss of her mother had a significant impact on her and she became severely depressed, eventually not even wanting to get out of bed. The three men were left to look after each other and Violet. It must have been a terrible shock to lose their mother so suddenly.

She was never the same after that. A few years later at age twenty-five she was admitted to Gladesville Mental Hospital, where she was eventually diagnosed with schizophrenia. She remained in mental hospitals and nursing homes for the rest of her life. My father visited her every fortnight, most of the time with his brother, Alec. I can see my father now, striding up the back cement path, which was lined with rose bushes, butting up against the usual parcel of lawn. There were trees along the fence line of our small back garden, a Hills hoist, and a rope swing from the nectarine tree. With his hat on and a bag of sweets for his sister under his arm, the gate clicked and he was off. It was ten minutes' walk up the hill, then two buses to get to Gladesville hospital, where he met Alec.

I knew about mental illness from an early age but I didn't really know what it was. It was shrouded in secrecy, it was a mystery. I asked my father many times if I could go with him on Saturday afternoons when he went to visit Violet but I was not allowed. I would ask my father about her but he said that my mother had told him that he was not to talk to me about her. When I eventually visited her, in my thirties, I met this lady whom I loved. She was a gentle soul much like my father. However, she did believe that she had built the Sistine Chapel. 'These are Holy hands,' she said, holding them out to show me.

Dad was always there. He never said 'I love you', which seems to be the trend today. In spite of that, if I was ever sure of anything, it was his love. Of course I was never able to say 'I love you' to him, yet I could not have loved anyone more. I am sure he knew. He gave me everything, his care, his concern, his wisdom, but most of all his love. He had a heart full of love.

One day we were visiting a friend in a psychiatric hospital. As we were walking along the corridor, a female patient approached my father and gently touched his sleeve. 'Please, sir, would you be careful not to step on the pile of baby's clothes,' pointing to a spot on the floor of the corridor.

'Yes, of course,' replied my father as he lifted his leg and carefully placed his foot down on the other side of the 'baby clothes'.

'Thank you,' she said. 'You are a gentleman.'

There he is! I can see him clearly. He is in the church hall among a crowd of parishioners dressed in a suit and tie as always, back straight. His hymn book is perched on the top of the piano and he stands beside it. I can hear his voice resonating with joy, singing the words of 'How great thou art'. Many people have told me over the years that they cannot hear that hymn without thinking of my dad. He was not frightened to show or speak of his faith but he knew how to do it. He lived his faith.

In the third verse where it says 'I see the brook', he would sing 'I see the broowk'. I can hear it now, his Irish accent, jerking at my tear ducts as if he were here. And the familiar strains of 'Danny Boy', a comforting world for me, bounded by 'Galway Bay', 'I'll take you home again Kathleen', and 'When Irish eyes are smiling'.

It is strange how both my brother and I both strived to be more like him, almost as if, by being so, it might have made up for my mother's vehement dislike of him. Now that he has gone, we talk about him often.

As I've suggested, my home life was fraught with disharmony. My mother was as distant and as distasteful to my father as it was possible to be. My father tried not to argue. There was no communication between them except mediated by us, as children, running messages from one to the other. 'Could you tell your father that dinner is ready?' and at the dinner table, 'Could you ask your father to pass the salt please?' Everything was communicated in that way.

When we had visitors, my mother would wait on them, bringing them cups of tea and coffee. She was a wonderful hostess. But she ignored my father. Usually some considerate – or more likely embarrassed – person would bring my father a cup of tea and something to eat. The majority of what my mother said to my father was negative and he learned for the most part not to respond. It was a losing battle.

They passed each other in the home like ships in the night, passing, never touching, never connecting; my mother was adept at avoiding any contact whatever with my father. There was a deathly hush over our home, a sense of foreboding. I felt it was my job to be on alert to listen for any sounds which were unexpected, and to be ready to act if necessary to prevent any catastrophe from occurring. Also I felt I needed to look after my brother, as I needed him. Without him, I would be truly alone. I had to sleep with one ear open and to be prepared. I'd had many instances to support my need to be vigilant. The luxury of quietly drifting into sleep was not there for me.

The walls of our house stood still around us watching, waiting, the silent spectators of our lives, our sadness etched into them for eternity. That was how things were. It was embarrassing for me when family or friends were there, as I am sure they thought things quite strange. Or maybe they didn't notice. Someone later told me that you could cut the atmosphere with a knife.

On weekends, I played in the back lane with the neighbourhood boys, as there were no girls. We rode billy carts down the steep slope of our back lane. Children made their own carts with the help of their parents, and there were many hills and slopes in Mosman where you could ride them. It was great fun. Every Saturday afternoon, I went to the pictures with Helen at the Orpheum Theatre in Cremorne. Her father was a friend of the manager and so she was allowed to get in free. I paid only sixpence, from memory. We saw some wonderful movies: *Brigadoon, Love is a Many Splendoured Thing, Cat on a Hot Tin Roof, The King and I, Rebel Without a Cause* and *Gidget*. We would see double features each time, as well as some cartoons, and the world news. Before it started, you had to stand up for 'God Save the Queen'. During the interval, a girl came around selling ice creams in a bucket, Jaffas, Fantales, and crisps. During the movie you would often hear Jaffas rolling down the aisles. The scrunching of lolly papers continued throughout the session.

Helen had two brothers. The older one, Reg, was six years older than Helen and I. He didn't know I existed but I fell in love with him. I thought he was gorgeous. Sometimes I wonder if he knew. It was a nice fantasy. A few years later, I went to see him in a production of *Jesus Christ Superstar*. It was amazing. Years after that, my mother went to see *Betty Blockbuster* with her friend Dorothy Venn. They were a little shocked, I heard via the grapevine. Reg Livermore was very well known by then, of course. My mother told me that Reg used to come to our house on his way home from school and he would perform his plays for her. She maintains she was his first audience.

My life continued on its way. We did the normal things – had breakfast, showered and got ready for school – the only difference being that in our house my parents did not ever speak to each other. At times my mother's loud shouting and banging of doors would startle me. Sometimes I was woken from sleep. Once when I heard the smashing of glass followed by dire threats, I feared that my father would be killed. For many years after, I continued to be frightened by loud voices, sudden noises and any arguments.

The neighbours couldn't have helped hearing everything, and I just wished that someone would do something. They never did. I thought that perhaps my teachers at high school might have said something, as I cried all the way to school, wiping my tears as I got to the school gate.

My childhood lasted a long time. I thought it would never end. I didn't want it to end, exactly, but I wanted something to happen. And things did, but just not the things I wished for.

I tried hard to please my mother. She loved my brother, I thought, but not me. I felt that I never measured up to her expectations. Not ever, in the way I dressed, spoke, acted or behaved.

Later, thankfully, I had a good relationship with my mother but that was not until I was almost sixty. By then I had learned to accept her as she was. She was fun, humorous and interesting in later life. Through the toughest times and all the tears – and there were many of them – through all the rejection, for she said some truly horrible things to me, I was determined that I would never give up.

The year of my leaving certificate was a difficult time. Trying to study in a household so far from normal was unimaginable. I studied from the time I got home from school until nine p.m. I was not allowed to stay up any later. With still more work to do, I set my alarm for a quarter to five and did some more work before school. In fact, it was fairly peaceful at night because my mother went to bed at seven-thirty and my father, after washing up, went to his room. He was not allowed to make a noise and neither was I, because it would wake my mother up. We didn't have a TV set because, when there was enough money to buy one, my mother bought one for my grandparents.

So, every night it was deathly quiet. I used to get down on the floor with my head as close to the speaker of my record player as I could, and play my records over and over. During those times, I had words in my head which went over and over, saying, 'Go on, kill yourself. Go on, kill yourself. Go on, do it.' To stop it, I used to whisper over and over to myself, very quietly so my mother could not hear. 'Please don't let them get me, please don't let them get me, please, please.' Part of me knew 'them' was her – but I must not or could not let her hear.

I talked to my father at times, but it was a risk to do so as we were forced to take sides. That is, we were both to support our mother, or we would surely pay. We were torn between the two and, to my chagrin, I was extremely rude to my father at one time in an effort to support my mother. It was a tightrope we walked. One friend who was there to see it told me later that she was shocked at my behaviour. The home situation worried me terribly. I did not feel like eating and was losing weight. I felt alone and very lonely, separated from normality.

### To Be Alone

To be alone, losing touch…no contact
Just to feel, to know, some one to share…
Sinking deeper, losing grip
If it breaks…then what?

The trees with gentle rhythm blowing
Enfold with care
Warmed by the sunshine they reach up
Where blue skies seem never ending

White clouds sail peacefully,
Contented, protected.
A gentle calm seems evident
As each blends and knows its part.

Is the love
Which God intended
To be found here?

Our house had two bedrooms and a fibro room built on at the back, where I slept. There was no central heating and it was freezing in my room. But often in winter I would turn on a small one-bar electric heater while I was studying. I sat almost on top of it in an effort to get warm, and on two occasions I fell asleep and when I woke I saw big blisters right up my leg from the heater. There were no blinds or curtains on the windows except for lightweight net see-through ones. The old man next door would peer at me through his laundry window. It was scary. My mother did not like blinds or curtains, just as she did not like doors. She took them all off and had two walls knocked out to make a long open space, well before open plan homes became popular.

My parents moved into separate rooms when I was about seven. After that, my brother no longer had a room to sleep in, so he had to sleep with my mother. When he was about ten or eleven, I kicked up a big fuss, because when my friends came they would ask, as children do, where I slept and where my brother slept. I dreaded those questions. Another question I got was about the rope clothes line stretched across the garden. I could not say, 'That's because my mother went to work and bought the Hills hoist, with her own money, so my father is not allowed to use it.' Instead I froze. He was not allowed to use the washing machine either, as my mother had bought that also, so every Saturday morning he would wash his clothes in the bath, wring them out and hang them on his rope clothes line. When it rained all weekend, it was a nightmare. I hated seeing my father treated like that and tried desperately to stand up for him, unsuccessfully. Listing all his good points to my mother was futile. For every good point, she would list several more bad points, and in very strong language no less.

Eventually, Helen's mother Dorothy must have realised our situation and gave us a divan for my brother to sleep on. For a while it was in the dining room, then in the sun room – a longer room, which was formerly an enclosed veranda. There were two doors leading into my room at the back, one to my brother's room, which was now my father's, and one to the back veranda. When it rained, it would pelt down onto the back veranda so that you would get wet going out to the toilet. It was scary; I thought someone could easily break into my room.

At weekends when I wandered the streets, I found peacefulness and tranquillity. There were no expectations. It was an escape, a haven, a refuge from uncertainty. The chorus of the Salvation Army song echoes perfectly the feelings that I experienced for many years. I listened to this and felt a calm, a peace.

**There will be God (by Marjorie Webb)**

Ten thousand years may pass away
And bring the dawning of a cosmic day
Age after age; time after time hold its sway

Man walks alone amid uncertainty
Only one thing can still make him strong
In the pain, in the doubt, in the loneliness
In the struggle of right against wrong
Somewhere amidst the confusion
There will be hope, there will be love, there will be God.

All time will pass into eternity
And man must venture on a life unknown
Journey alone, each to his destiny.

Man walks alone amidst uncertainty
Only one thing can still make him strong
In the pain, in the doubt, in the loneliness
In the struggle of right against wrongs
Somewhere amidst the confusion
There will be hope, there will be love, and there will be God.

# 3

My mother went to work during the day. At night she cooked our dinner and my dad always washed up. After dinner she would lie on her bed with the evening paper stretched out on her lap. Following that she would run a hot bath. After a day at work, it must have been relaxing for her. Then she would go to bed. That was her routine. Meanwhile, my father would be doing the dishes in the kitchen and I would take the opportunity to talk to him while I dried the dishes.

In the morning she was up early – by a quarter to five. She would first make herself a cup of coffee and read the morning paper, the *Sydney Morning Herald*, from cover to cover, sitting in front of the stove in the kitchen, after she had turned on the oven or the griller to keep her warm. She never wore slippers or socks in the house to keep her feet warm, just her dressing gown and always bare feet, until the day she died.

When she was in and out of hospital, in her last years, the nurses kept asking her, 'Emma, haven't you got any slippers?'

'No,' she would say. 'What would I want those for?'

She felt the cold so much that it was surprising that she didn't keep her feet warm. She would not wear warm clothes, as she wanted to look well dressed; cardigans and jumpers made you look 'frumpy'. She could not bear the tracksuits often worn by older women her own age. A fashion designer or beauty consultant had told her never to put cardigans, coats or jackets on top of a lovely outfit and if you were cold to wear a spencer, or other such item under the outfit. And so she dressed that way, even when it was bitterly cold, while everyone else was wearing coats and scarves. But you could see her outfit and that was the important thing.

However, I remember one or two evenings while she was waiting in Crown Street, where the orchestra that I was in held rehearsals, probably to collect me from the bus after a trip away. It was winter and the wind was whipping the sides of the buildings. On that day, she was wearing her brown fur-like coat. It still exists. I have it in my wardrobe and may wear it one day. It is probably more than fifty years old.

My mother was her own person, a woman ahead of her time, with intelligence, dreams, compassion, and she worked hard to do what she could to help those less fortunate than herself. She truly wished the best for those people. A country girl, born and bred, she had benefited from the country life. She loved her dad; he was her hero, her model of manhood and she was to measure every man in her life against him. He adored her, but of all his daughters she was the one he feared for most. My father told me that he would go to her house when they were courting and she would be playing the piano, and crying. He said he always wondered why. When she was about twelve years of age, her brother, aged eight, died of encephalitis and her mother, my grandmother, took to her bed. My mother said that she often did not have clean underwear, and because of the extra jobs she was required to do, she was often late for school. As she had missed so much schooling due to being in quarantine, she was forced to leave school early. I suspect that the death of her brother had a great impact on the family. She would never talk about it.

She had many ideas for helping people: underprivileged children, the elderly and all who were disadvantaged in any way. Her vision was for the church to provide an opportunity for underprivileged children from the country 'who had never seen the ocean' to have a holiday there. She went to work voluntarily each weekend, at Vision Valley. This was a camp site and conference centre that was operated by the Central Methodist Mission, Sydney. It was on a huge property west of Sydney. Accommodation was provided in modern wooden cottages that would accommodate several people in each. The aim was to provide a place that schools, institutions or groups could use for conferences, holidays or a break.

In later years, she worked for the Central Methodist Mission, travelling by ferry into the city, and then a bus ride up Pitt Street.

She spent most of her day on the phone talking to the brothers at the Catholic schools and colleges and telling them of the possibilities for them and the boys in their schools. Her mode of working was person to person, on the phone initially, and after that she would take the Brothers out for afternoon tea. They would talk over and plan for their various needs over a Devonshire tea, which she would always pay for. She was passionate in all that she did. While she was in charge of that area, the church was making a significant profit. When she left, at age seventy-four, they replaced her with two people and a computer. But computers, of course, are not personable, and so the church lost a considerable amount of money. It was the face-to-face contact, the building up of a relationship with the clients, that was the key. My mother knew that; she was a natural at the work. Eventually, all but one of the conference centres closed.

Her favourite place for coffee was the little café at Mosman Wharf, a tiny coffee shop run by an Italian (or was he Greek?) and his wife. He knew how to make good coffee. My mother used to make percolated coffee in the fifties and she really appreciated her cup of coffee. When coffee shops opened in Sydney in the city, she would go shopping on a Saturday morning and have her raisin toast and a cappuccino. At the wharf she would sit in a seat near the water, beside a window where the sun was pouring through, as she loved the sun. The café comprised a tiny kitchen leading out to a tongue-shaped area filled with tables and chairs. The aroma of freshly brewed coffee and bacon and eggs permeated the area.

The wharf was alive with activity on weekday mornings. She would go there early, every morning during the week, at one stage. There were people who were waiting for the next ferry, sitting quietly reading the paper, others doing business over breakfast, as the constant flow of workers passed by, coming off or embarking on the ferry to Circular Quay. The workers streamed past. I am sure they appreciated the smell of coffee and hot breakfasts cooking as they filed onto the ferry.

What a joy life was in Sydney. To be close to the water of Sydney

Harbour and to ride on the water, experiencing the surrounds of the Harbour Bridge and the elements, was and is a privilege. It was a bit different in winter when the rain bucketed down. No one wanted to sit outside on the ferry on those days. Now, when I do the ferry trip when I return to Sydney, I think how fortunate I was to have lived in such a beautiful city. Perhaps when you live there you become blasé about the natural beauty of the place and treat a ferry ride merely as a mode of transport.

My mother's married life began in 1940, near Cremorne Wharf where the newly-weds had rented a flat, at first a fully serviced one, for the honeymoon period, then the normal rental accommodation for that time. My mother told of the first meal after the wedding, which she cooked meticulously, meat and vegetables, and placed on the table with pride in front of my Irish father. 'What! No potatoes?' he said. She had forgotten the potatoes, and she told me later that she was devastated. She retold this story again before she died at ninety-one and a half.

Life must have been precarious in those days. She remembered when the Japanese submarine came into Sydney Harbour; it must have been terrifying. She told me that my father was very frightened and they both hid under the dining table. Coming from Belfast with all its fighting, and thinking Australia a safe destination, it must have been unexpected for him. He told me that on one occasion in his youth, just after curfew, he narrowly escaped being shot. He was crossing the road that divided the Protestant and the Roman Catholic areas.

I guess it takes a lifetime to piece everything together and extract the goodness from the grain. She looked after her mother and father extremely well. She went to work in order to be able to buy a TV set for them, as she thought my grandfather, in particular, would enjoy watching some of the programs. She was diligent in her adherence to the fifth commandment and the promise proved right, as she lived a long life. My grandparents wanted for nothing, while my brother and I, in about 1958, used to watch parts of TV shows in shop windows and I watched *Wagon Train* each week at a friend's house. Interestingly,

I did not have a television set myself till about twenty years later, when my first child was five years old. However, I only began to watch and enjoy programs after I retired. It was a whole new experience.

Recently, my auntie told me, or reminded me, that my mother had not wanted to marry my dad and that one day she rang her father to say that she wanted to get a divorce. We were very young; I was probably about six years of age. He discouraged her, so my father later told me, saying that she would be shunned. Divorce was frowned on in those days. My auntie also told me that my mother always had a real temper. I knew. One day she was so angry with Dad that she smashed all the dishes in the kitchen cupboard. I was so frightened. I remember it well. I rang my Nanna and said, 'Come down quickly. Things are really bad.' It took a while, as she needed to get two buses to get to our house. In those days, fewer people had cars.

I remember that Dr Holmes came to our house to talk to my parents. My brother and I were locked outside and I was very scared. We could see and hear them through the kitchen window, shouting and screaming. I disliked Dr Holmes intensely. I guess I blamed him for interfering. But it was also because he seemed to me so pompous. However, it was significant that my parents did have some counselling, of a sort. The following quote from Dorothy Rowe's book *Beyond Fear* describes exactly how I felt:

> When a small child is presented with events which he cannot master because there are no explanations which he can understand or accept, and because the parents neither recognize that the child is distressed, nor seek to comfort and reassure him, then the child is in peril of being overwhelmed and his fragile sense of self, annihilated. In this situation one desperate defence the child can use is to take the whole experience inside him. He cannot distance himself from it, for it is too vast and all encompassing, and too important to him. It becomes part of himself, part of his fantasies and nightmares, part of his very 'self'.
>
> This is the process by which many of us 'inherit' depression. We take in our mother's depression, and carry within us images of darkness, despair and murderous rage – not our own but our mother's.

Our home had so many bad and unhappy memories locked within its walls that sometimes I used to feel the happy ones were not enough to compensate. Every corner of the house I grew up in, every inch of its being, was saddened by the events of the years. I saw sadness wherever I looked, I heard tears from every corner, and I felt anxiety, insecurity and loneliness lurking in every room. There was no real privacy in our house; in fact, I could never relax even in my own room, knowing anyone could walk in at any time.

Life did not change so much, it seemed, as a child. Awakening in the morning, the routine was the same for many years. I woke to the sound of a massed chorus of birds, which I could see from my window, through the flimsy, net curtains. There was frost on the windows and that made them a little more dense. They were big windows in my room on each wall; you had to push them outwards and hook up a handle to keep the window open. Out of this window I could see Mr Kaski's house. I looked out onto his laundry, and he and I looked at each other quite often, it seemed. His eyes appeared big when the light in my room illuminated them. He could see everything when the lights were on. He was quite scary to me, an old man then in his eighties and a bit senile. When I looked out into the darkness and saw his face in the window, I was frightened. It was as if he was spying on me; he was always there. Eventually I used to get down on the floor to study, where I hoped that he could not see me. I had no privacy in my home and so it was in the open-air daylight on my walks that I felt my privacy.

Later, as a teenager, I used to listen to records on the floor with my head in my hands to shut out the world. It didn't work. Fear began for me as child. The feelings are still with me; just a trigger is all that's needed to spark it off and then it all comes back, as though it lives in me, and me with it; it and I are in the same body. I carry it. I house it, and it is within me and towers over me, as it did in the past. But now it works in a different way, a more positive one.

**Peace**

Peacefulness within
Calm, a quiet stillness
Honesty and truth I offer you,
Is it love?

Deep within I sense a need to live out
An unfulfilled hope
To have found at death the richness of life within
Unique, meaningful, a God-given identity.

To ignore it would be a rejection of a
Divine purpose
To love, perhaps to be, to simply live,
But love cannot break through the fetters of an encased identity

I thought he was dead. I was fifteen. I walked into her bedroom and there he was, lying on the bed. Not moving. He was fully dressed in his school uniform, with boater, shirt, tie, blazer, socks and shoes. My brother. My mother had put him there. Presumably as a joke: she did have a good sense of humour. But this…well, it was just too much. It took me more than a few seconds to realise that it was a dummy, but my heart was pounding.

Another time, a couple of years earlier, she hid in the wardrobe in my room – unbelievable but true. My two friends at high school, Heather Barrett and Carole Enge, had come to my house after school. It was probably the only time I remember a friend coming home apart from my friend, Helen. We were thirteen, in our first year of high school. We were in the bedroom chatting, having had afternoon tea, all sitting on the bed. It was comfortable, it was nice, and I had two friends whom I liked and who liked me and we were spending time together. I felt happy almost, secure in myself, and able to share the confidences typical of young teenagers. We had been there for a while and we were discussing important issues, our feelings, our concerns, fully trusting each other.

Suddenly there was a loud noise. Out of my wardrobe jumped my mother. She was laughing. I was paralysed with fear, embarrassed, and concerned for my friends. I no longer felt safe. I now knew that my mother had heard all of our conversations.

Years later while recalling old memories together, my mother suddenly said, 'Remember the time I hid in your wardrobe. You and your friends were sitting on the bed together?' Glancing at me she noticed the look on my face. 'But it was just a joke,' she said.

Fear began for me as a young child: fear of loud noises, such as raised voices, crashing glass, or doors being slammed. The latter signalled that an argument between my parents was in full swing, as did a certain intonation of voice, or shouting and screaming, accompanied by banging and threats of violence. 'I'll get even with you, I'd like to stick a knife in you.' This caused extreme anxiety and feelings of panic in me, fear, that is, of what might happen, of being annihilated, of being hurt, abandoned or of just being left alone.

### A Fear of Anger

Take a hundred clanging cymbals
And a host of beating drums
And play them surrounded by panes of glass
To see what it might do
My heart is like the glass I fear
It shakes and quivers too
That one day that cymbal crash – *fortissimo*!
Will shatter all the panes of glass
Perhaps even me…

Fear brings with it a sense of insecurity and exposure, a longing for silence, and for peace and the restoration of balance to one's world. Fear rocks your equilibrium; for me, I was displaced into a sort of 'foreign' land where nothing was predictable, where in fact no one was safe and, furthermore, the ones who should have been doing the protecting were the ones committing the acts that produced full-blown panic. I would freeze, cut off, and find a quiet place within myself to rest until calm was restored. I fashioned an ideal place in a real safe haven that I discovered.

**Trees**

The reflection of trees in the water
So clearly the image is mirrored,
Then the water is stirred and the ripples begin,
The image begins to quiver and shake.

All is quiet once more and peacefulness restored.
The image of the trees stands straight and clear,
Just so the beauty of life is reflected in a face
Which shows warmth and love aglow.
Serene though it seems it will often be disturbed
By the stresses and strains it receives.

The clear image in the water returns.
God shows his love to us it seems,
Through pain and sorrow, and through those who have known
That to live is to suffer
To find God – He appears in love.

My brother and I looked forward to my mother arriving home from work, as she always brought home some treats. Of course, at thirteen or fourteen years of age, it was not a good time to be eating sweets and cakes, but that didn't matter. We enjoyed them as it was a real treat for afternoon tea, one bonus, perhaps, of having a working mother. So, bearing delicious cakes and pastries from the Greek cake shop near Flinders Street in Darlinghurst, where her office was now located, she came striding down the garden path. As she walked, I could hear her high heels clicking on the cement. She was elegant, her handbag hanging from one elbow, her car keys in the other hand. I could sometimes tell from her footsteps how stressful her day had been. Fast steps, click click click, short, sharp and purposeful: it had been a busy day, and she was happy. If they were slower, longer steps, or softer clicks, carrying along her sadness in their wake, it was not a good day. On days like that, the phone would likely ring several times. I just knew it.

Almost every afternoon, it seemed, as soon as she walked in the door, the phone would ring. It was as if he knew exactly how long it took for her to get home. She would then be on the phone for an hour or so. Sometimes she would hang up and a few minutes later the phone would ring again. If I wanted to talk to her, I would walk in and out, hoping to catch her gaze, her attention, hoping she would put down the phone to look at me. She never did.

But for me, much worse than that was hearing the sad, anguished tone of her voice in response to an obviously fraught conversation that was being carried on with the person on the other end of the phone. She was unhappy, desperately unhappy.

My strongest and most poignant memory of her in my childhood is of her sitting in a big old-fashioned light green lounge chair, soft and comfortable, sobbing her heart out, tears pouring down her cheeks. I went up to her and tried to comfort her, to give her a hug, but she pushed me away. After a while, in order to avoid rejection, I stopped doing it.

**Love**

To receive love and to give it
To need and to be needed
The pain and fear it brings
Of mixed longings and yearnings
And of the growth that needs to be done.

In accepting the love that is given
And loving in return
Is to feel a person worthwhile
Yet sometimes to feel so alone.

To take a risk and get to know you,
To find warmth so accepting and real,
The understanding of suffering and pain
That has to be endured, is to feel closeness,
An affinity that makes life seem more real.

For to share one's needs and longings
Is to be aware of oneself
Of the fears and the longings within
And the need to be understood.

To love someone as a person
Is to love them in more ways than one
To allow them to have many feelings
And to accept them, each one.

To be loved as a child
To be allowed to nurture care and comfort
And to be comforted in return
Is to feel a whole person.

The expression of love is endless
But the meaning of it is true
That it is in the giving and receiving
That makes life so worthwhile.

To love someone is a privilege
And then to be loved in return…
Such a feeling of acceptance and humanness
Is yours for a moment in time.

To hang on to it is foolish
For life goes on its way
But the memory of moments of closeness
And oneness will always remain.

In those days, she smoked cigarettes. It wasn't as acceptable for women to smoke in those days. Moreover, it was most unacceptable to me. The two men in her office chain-smoked. The atmosphere was overpowering; needless to say, it was difficult to breathe. That was in 1950. It was my mother's first job after having children. It was called Hillman-Humber Spare Parts, an automobile business located at 188 George Street. The office was dingy and cluttered and of no interest to me. There were ashtrays all over the desks in between greasy old car parts which overflowed everywhere. It was chaos. I think that my mother must have given up trying to keep it tidy and clean. What she did do, on a regular basis, was to tip the alcohol down the sink at any opportunity. One of the men was an alcoholic. Possibly that was the reason that he rang to speak to her every afternoon, crying on the phone. I just knew when it was him; I could tell by the tone of her voice. I was thirteen then and I felt disloyal to my father. Did he know? I dislike alcohol now, having seen the devastating effect it can have on people's lives and those of their children and everyone around them.

My guess is it was in that office my mother began smoking. I took every opportunity to beg her to stop. Her overwhelming unhappiness permeated our house, it settled in the walls and in the furniture. She was so far trapped in the sadness that there appeared to be no hope. Ironic though it was, she persuaded me to start smoking when I was twenty-one, although I protested bitterly. She convinced me that it would make me feel better.

The quiet soft conversations on the phone continued for years, lengthy ones which stopped briefly, or became softer, when I came into the room, and my fears mounted, thinking that something terrible was going to happen, especially when my mother took my brother and me out with 'the man in the office' on his sailing boat. I was not happy about it; the whole time I was there I was feeling very upset for my father. It took time, years of time, for whatever was to happen, but nothing did.

My father once accused her of being in love with 'the man in the office'. She denied it. I thought she was in love with him, and consequently I disliked him. 'The man in the office' became part of our lives; if help or support was needed, it was to him that she turned.

Eventually his business partner died, and so it was just my mother and Mr Horsfield in the office. And his dog. I disliked it too. I still do not like cocker spaniels. We had to get a cocker spaniel puppy because he had one. I felt that I had to pretend that I liked his dog, and its owner. It was a lie.

She worked in that office for seventeen years, and would never take holidays. He could not do without her. He gave her gifts, a piano, a radiogram, a washing machine and numerous other things to make up for all the missed holidays over the years. Every year another gift appeared, much to my father's disgust and anger.

I remember my father trying many times to persuade her to give up work. In his opinion, she didn't need to work. But he put up with it, even balancing the books for her each month, for which he was paid a pittance. I believe he still loved her, thus he continued to support her, believing he had no other option. I remember these weekends when the books were being done. It took the whole weekend. I went out walking for most of it. I remember the frustration and the hours they spent trying to find the penny that they could not account for. 'I'll give you the penny,' I said. 'Here – now you won't have to look for it.' I never did understand bookkeeping.

Sometimes on the weekend my mother used to take my brother and me to 'wander'. My father was not invited to come with us. She would not go out with him. It was a drive, to here there and everywhere, to exciting and different places. Usually we ended up at Manly, though. We would listen to the Salvation Army band, which played on the corso every Sunday afternoon. I loved the drums and the big booming voice of the captain singing, 'Wide Wide as the Ocean', holding his arms out wide to indicate.

> Wide wide as the ocean,
> High as the heavens above,
> Deep deep as the deepest sea,
> Is my Saviour's love?
> I though so unworthy,
> Still am a child of his care.
> For his word teaches me.
> That his love reaches me
> Everywhere.

After the service, they gave out little coloured texts which I loved. These were so small that you could hold them in the palm of your hand, and they had lovely pictures on them that were beautifully coloured. I saved them and treasured them.

The atmosphere in our house was one of extremes. At night there was silence, complete silence and quietness, so as not to wake my mother. At the other extreme there was loud and violent shouting, hysterical screaming, smashing of things and kicking of doors. At that point, my father would put on his hat and walk out the door. He came back later when things had hopefully calmed down. It did not help us as children. We were left in a scary place.

It was lonely, waiting to be shown affection; at least that is what I felt, for as long as I could remember. I remember being in my fibro room, looking out the window that I once smashed my fist through, at the hydrangeas that got watered every Sunday morning along with my windows, to wake us up. My mother was always up at a quarter to five in the morning. The nectarine tree was out the window too, the one I used to climb and hang from its branches by my legs. I remember staring out the window feeling the uttermost loneliness and despair. It was one of those times that I smashed my fist through the window. My hand needed stitches, and the window…well, it shattered.

But what I did know was that God was with me and He would never let me down. I believed that and I never lost that faith.

**Alone**

If I were to curl in a tight little ball
That it could not hurt me ever at all,
For the fear it could ever break me in two,
Perhaps destroy me – I think it could do.

The big empty hole filled with fear and pain,
Comes back again and there remains,
I wish it would go –
Please, just leave me alone –
For a while to feel I am whole again.

If I stand on the sand and watch the waves
Gently flow out to sea –
Part of me is breaking, tearing apart –
Part of me here – and part of me there.

I can but love,
The most wonderful gift,
That God should have known
How to reach what's adrift.
With a power so mighty, so great that He
Could have given it to me and to you.

At night we would sit around the cream wooden table with flaps on each side to extend the table to seat four people. With one flap up, it made a rectangle when the long edge was pushed to the wall. Initially, my mother and father sat at each end and we were on stools on the long end, which meant that we could kick each other under the table and feed scraps of unwanted food to the dog. We played games at night: I Spy, Countries and Capitals, and Animal, Vegetable or Mineral. Our mother was very quick and livened up these games with her sense of fun. In later years, my father ate alone. My mother liked it that way. It was how she planned it. It was sad for us. 'But where's Dad?' we would ask. 'Oh, he's working back,' she would say.

I loved Sunday nights. I remember the smell of cut grass as people mowed their lawns on the weekend, often on Sunday afternoons. I used to play with the children in the street, enjoying their companionship, the freedom and the open air. Tea was tinned spaghetti on toast in front of the gas fire. There was a sense of security and comfort derived from those times. After tea, my mother would peel three or four big shiny oranges full of juice, and cut them up into quarters. But my brother would usually ask her to cut a 'door' in the top of his.

When my brother was about ten, he decided that he wanted to learn to play the drum. My father took him and me to the city on a Saturday morning to the old Palings building in Angel Place. On the first floor, which you reached by a rickety old-fashioned lift, there was a huge studio used for orchestra rehearsals and other events. Sid Verey was seated at a table with two of his young students who were just finishing their lesson. There were playing on round ribbed rubber mats on the table with Premier drumsticks; there were no real drums to learn on. I did not like 'Golden Wedding' and the jazz drumming that Mr Verey taught, but I was fascinated by the marches my brother was learning. In due course, he tired of drum lessons but I was keen to learn. From then on, my father took me to drum lessons every Saturday morning. In the big studio where lessons were held, a youth orchestra called the National Youth Symphony Orchestra of Australia rehearsed every Friday night. The players were aged from fifteen to twenty-five. Later it was the BMC (British Motor Corporation) NYSO, as they then were the sponsors. They played classical music, which I loved.

When I joined the percussion section, there were two boys, Ross aged thirteen and Billy who was twelve. I was fourteen when I joined. Billy was the youngest in the orchestra. The orchestra was to be my main love for the next eight or so years of my life. It was very special for me, a joy that was to be part of my life for years to come; and, indeed, my enjoyment of the music would last a lifetime.

We had concerts in the Sydney Town Hall and in various other locations in Sydney, as well as travelling by bus to several country towns in New South Wales including Orange, Bathurst and Cooma, where we were billeted with families. It was all very exciting. My father would sit through the rehearsals every Friday night, watching and listening to the music, sometimes reading the paper. For him, it was just as much a special time. He loved the music and it was an opportunity for us to spend time together. Needless to say, he never attended one of the concerts. Whenever there were concerts, my mother was always the one to go, and of course they would never go out anywhere together. Such was the way of our family.

Music has always been a part of my life. Both of my parents loved classical music. My father was an accountant with the ABC, and music was very much part of the scene. My mother had attended free orchestral concerts from the age of thirteen. In those days, she walked to Campsie station and got the train to Town Hall station so that she could attend the free Sunday afternoon concerts held in Sydney Town Hall.

Towards the end of her life, my mother was more peaceful. Her last two days were particularly happy. She had decided that it was time for her to go, telling my brother and me that she had 'ticked all the boxes'. I think she may still have been a little disappointed and perhaps she had hoped for more. But we could not have known what she wanted. She would never have told us directly. In her last days, I know that she appreciated her room, and the people caring for her. I do miss her. Now.

# Part Two

# 4

> Love I could never reach, love in its self knowledge, love that does not alter 'where it alteration finds'. Just moments, seconds, of vague comprehension, then the inevitable shuddering away into perversity, chaos. Love, responsibility to souls, is still leagues beyond my ken.
>
> Francis Webb, writing to Rosemary Dobson, despairing of his lack of friends, and the fact that he would be in hospital for life

It was all very scary being admitted to a psychiatric hospital. I was nineteen, and very naive. However, I was so sick that at least it felt like something was going to be done to help me. The details of how I arrived there are hazy and mostly long forgotten but I do remember my mother taking me to the hospital.

At that stage, I had been seeing a psychiatrist called Dr Stephen for some time, as an outpatient. But after the incident in Kiama it was decided that I needed hospitalisation. Maybe now someone will help me, I thought. It was a dark place, and I had not been there before.

**Darkness**

Out there in the darkness so often I see
The light of a rainbow but not for me
For I can't quite catch it – it slips right away
Lest something should snap, that way to remain.

Warm as the sun, so safe and secure
How can I cease to yearn for it now
That feeling of love that surrounds just a child,
Seems a rare and a priceless treasure to find.

Fear surrounds and encases the one
Who seeks to find a reason for life
But the love and warmth, which God does show
Is alive in the beauty around me now.

Yet to find that love,
A crippling desire,
It chokes and stifles, and causes such pain,
Let it go…maybe to come again

A reason for life I'm sure there must be.
For around me things of such beauty I see
Yet darkness and pain comes back and remains
No wonder the question is life for me.

To leave this life would be a release
A blessed feeling of peace
To drift away from the empty hole
At the bottom, there must be a light.

Gently the wind blows through the trees
Sways and rocks their boughs.
It seems to say there is a way,
Just keep on searching, tho' the gusts they may blow.

    I had never been in hospital before. In fact, I had never been sick. Arriving at the front door of the hospital was all very strange and unfamiliar. It had been an old house, which was converted some years before to be used as a psychiatric hospital by the Central Methodist Mission. The matron, Betty Anderson, took me to the room that was to be mine. Strangely enough, when she met us at the door, it turned out that she had known my mother in their younger days, when they attended the same church. That was of some comfort to my mother. At least, at first it was. I was put into a three-bed room. My bed was the one against the wall as you came in the door. My doctor had decided that I was to have insulin treatment, beginning the following morning. The other two people in my room were also having insulin, and had been for some time.

The next morning when I woke, it was to hear footsteps coming along the corridor. And at once the sister or nurse on duty arrived in our room. 'No breakfast this morning, girls, and you can keep your pyjamas on,' and she was gone. This was all very unsettling. I had no idea what to expect. We were all given our injections. I was given eighty units of insulin on one occasion, as I remember. If this is correct, then it was a very big dose. The aim was to put the patient into a coma for a few hours. On awakening, you would be given two to three glasses of glucose to drink in order to bring you out of the coma. I would wake up feeling very shaky and unsteady on my feet. I walked to the dining room, where we were told to sit down and drink our glucose. That was followed by lunch.

Sitting at the table with my glass of glucose in front of me, I felt very woozy. My vision seemed to be blurred and I had a strange feeling of being there but not able to participate. Once the glucose had been drunk, your body started to pick up, but it was still a while before you felt better. In addition to the insulin therapy I was to be given ECT twice weekly. Suddenly I was put upside down in my bed, not having been told very much at all, and then I was asked whether I had false teeth. This threw me into no-man's-land. I was so scared. False teeth? I was only nineteen.

**In the Dark**

In the depths of a dark black cavern
Right down there in the pit
Is a feeling of terror and fear,
trying to struggle to the top.

Strength is needed but weakness prevails
Knees give way as when walking in sand,
The warmth of the sun is all around
Yet to reach it?

I was not consulted about the treatment but I guess my parents were, as I was under twenty-one.

I lay in my bed, hearing the doctor's footsteps behind me, walking, then stopping to talk, more footsteps, as he and his nurse attended to the other patients in the queue, all lying upside down in their beds waiting. The big trolley full of heavy equipment was wheeled in. You could hear it trundling along the length of the room and stopping at each bed until it got to yours. You were given an injection of course – this was the sixties, and so treatment was more humane than it had been in the past. You would not know what happened – at least, you would not remember – but all the same you heard the sounds issuing from the treatments given to those who came before you, and that was quite disturbing.

It did work, the ECT, according to the doctors and reports from patients. But when you are on such a massive dose of medication, it is hard to know. I still felt very unwell. The worst part was the disorientation and the loss of memory. After having the treatment, I could not remember things, and on one occasion, on weekend leave while shopping with my mother in the local shopping centre, I met some girls from my school. They said hello, and chatted away to me. I had no idea who they were; I had no memory of them at all and had to act as if I did. My mother was there and helped as best she could.

They say it doesn't affect your memory and it is true that most of it comes back. Unfortunately for me, I forgot all the Latin I had learned at school and university. My French, I remembered, and still remember much of it, but I was a Latin teacher, so that was the end of that.

Time seemed endless in hospital, like a piece of elastic stretching out into nothingness. No signposts on this pathway to the future, and the future looked like a long time coming. For us, there were no worries in that we were freed from day-to-day concerns, and we were well looked after in our sanctuary. Life consisted of making sense of the hospital environment. And so we watched and learned, noticing each movement, each facial expression from the nurses, which might afford us some information. A furrowed brow could mean, 'She is a worry, you know, we should let doctor know. Maybe for treatment in the morning.' A smile, 'You are doing well, dear.'

We knew that we were being discussed, plans were being made, and we tried to extract from the body language of the staff, the doctors and nurses who they were for, and for what. Over their cups of tea and coffee and plates of delicious cakes they would make things called 'discharge plans', of which we had no knowledge. It was all a mystery to us.

Marianna was a patient who was there with me, younger, prettier and able to capture more of the longed-for attentions of Dr Stephen, dressed in his black suit, starched white shirt, and tie, a short portly man with a strong Scottish brogue and a comforting smile. We were beholden to him. He would decide our future, as surely as if he were God.

We waited around on the sunny verandas overlooking the lush garden beds of the suburban Sydney establishment which held within it the potential futures of thirty or so, mostly young, quite ill, patients. Most of the patients smoked; it was the pastime of psychiatric patients then, as it is still today. It filled the time and relaxed the tension within.

We longed for our doctor to smile, make eye contact, giving credence to the fact that in spite of the circumstances we were still part of the human race. I was never greeted first by the doctor; he might have managed to give me a cursory glance before writing in his notes that I was perhaps, 'attention-seeking and needy'.

I studied with all my energy the faces of the nurses, and at the appropriate times would question them. 'Can you tell me what's wrong with me?'

I received the time-worn responses. 'Oh no, dear. You'll have to ask doctor that. He'll be here soon. Run along now. You don't need to worry.'

'But sister, do I have schizophrenia?'

'Well, dear, probably most of the nurses here do, but you don't.'

With a laugh, and hoping that it was enough to satisfy me, she turned on her heel and departed speedily. And so back I went to a sunny spot in the garden where I could watch and wonder, until next called by the bell for 'pill time'. We waited in a long line to be given our pills and we were watched while we took them. It was all part of the routine.

Marianna was fascinating to me, gorgeous, attractive, vibrant, though she was very ill. She was being treated with LSD, which could be prescribed at the time but was ceased soon after. She would tell us stories of her experience under LSD. Colourful visions of beautiful places, and yet, at times, she looked extremely disturbed. I wanted it too. That way you could get more of the doctor's time. After all, he was the keeper of the key, although he only visited the hospital twice a week.

'Hello, Trish. And how are you feeling today?'

I would struggle to put into words the anguish within, by which time I realised that his attention was taken by one of the other patients waiting in my peripheral vision.

'Well, it's good that you're feeling a bit better.'

(I hadn't said that.)

'We will continue with the treatment. See you next week.' And then he was off, his shiny, black, polished shoes tapping the cement path as he swiftly made his way to the next patient.

Another patient, Alan, the same age as me, was very friendly and pleasant. I had no knowledge of relationships with the opposite sex so that when he pulled me into the bathroom as I came around the corner, and kissed me, I was totally overwhelmed and slapped him. Oh, the naiveté about life! It was pathetic. He was a very nice young man. Many years later I heard that he had been shot and killed by a gunman while working at a petrol station.

For six weeks I lived in this three-bed ward. Positioned as I was in the bed nearest the door, I was the first to hear the footsteps of the nurses each morning. I could see out the window opposite. Another patient lived under the window, and the third along the other wall.

There were small cupboards there, and a small side table. An old home, Federation style, it had a reasonably homely feel about it.

Every morning when I woke up and realised where I was, I dreaded the sound of the footsteps of the clinical nurse and her announcement of those who were for 'shock treatment' that morning. Staff were then busy moving around getting beds ready for the treatments. Lying there, hearing the ECT trolley rumbling along toward my room, I dreaded to hear my name called, and to be told, 'You're for ECT today.'

We usually went home for weekend leave, remembering to take our glucose with us. On one of my weekend leaves, I had forgotten to take mine with me. After lunch, feeling tired, I lay down and went to sleep. After some time, my mother was unable to wake me. I was supposed to be given my glucose and the following should not have happened. However, on the advice of my psychiatrist, my mother phoned an ambulance, and I was taken back to Waddell House. The doctor was to meet us there. He told me that he had fun speeding through the traffic while blowing the horn. I probably disturbed his peaceful Saturday afternoon.

Mental illness is a lonely existence. You can't really talk to normal people about it. They don't want to know. And of course most can't relate to it. After my first hospitalisation at Waddell House, I went back home as I'd had to leave Kiama High School. It was strange. I was on a lot of drugs and still seeing the psychiatrist but unable to talk to friends about what had happened. I never did. My best friend in the orchestra said, some time later, that she asked her mother if it was possible for someone to disappear off the face of the earth. When she rang, my mother would not tell her where I was, and so virtually no one visited me. That was how it was in those days; it was all hush-hush.

Mother came every day, much to the disapproval of the psychiatrist, who tried to stop her. She would meet me in the laneway down the back. My father came once or twice, but it was very hard for him, as public transport would have been impossible, and my mother would not let him drive the car.

I was unable to go to orchestra rehearsals for quite some time and it was hard to make up plausible reasons regarding my absence. I learned to fudge the truth. Nobody knew where I had been or what was wrong. Nobody in those days knew how to cope with mental illness. You just didn't talk about it.

At the end of June 1963, when I was well enough, I went to work at Blackfriars Correspondence School in Chippendale, not far from Sydney University. It was where teachers were sent who, for various reasons, medical or otherwise, were unable to cope with teaching in a normal school. Initially I was put in the high school section and given the students who were taking Latin. After a few weeks, it became apparent to me that I had forgotten most of the Latin that I had learned and loved for many years. I had to accept that I could no longer teach in my preferred area. The only option for me was to teach a primary class, and so I was given grade three primary school. It took me a while to learn and adjust to but for a while, things went well. I enjoyed the company of the other teachers and my supervisor was very good. It was not for long, though; I was there from the end of June 1963 until August of that year, when I left on sick leave.

The symptoms of my illness once again affected my work. My supervisor was very kind and patient in putting up with me, as it could not have been easy. I used to shake all the time, probably due to the medication. It was difficult to adjust to the new environment. However, it would have happened wherever I worked. The anxiety increased and the panic attacks become more frequent, and I became depressed once more. I remained at Blackfriars for the next few years, although I was often away on sick leave. Nothing was normal about my life – I felt cut off from the normal world and it was sheer misery. Sue Cattell, my best friend then and now, also a teacher at Blackfriars, was sent to go after me when I ran from the room. The teachers at the school, my supervisor and Jack, the man I helped in the printing and collating room, were extremely supportive. But they could not continue supporting me; I was almost certainly the most difficult person they had to deal with.

Normally, people at the correspondence school were there due to physical problems rather than psychiatric ones. In fact, after I was retired from teaching on medical grounds, the New South Wales Teachers Federation totally overhauled their entry requirements, realising that they needed to screen prospective students for psychiatric disorders. They took responsibility for the fact that it had not been picked up when I was accepted for teachers' college and I was granted a pension until I recovered.

Dr Stephen advised me, after more than a year and two hospitalisations without improvement, that he could not do anything more for me. He told me that there were 'nice little units' where I could live and be looked after. I was outraged and responded with what I regarded as righteous indignation. No doubt, it was then I picked up that he thought I had schizophrenia. I found out much later that my mother had been told that but she would not accept it.

Dr Stephen was still my psychiatrist, and I was seeing him regularly. But I think he was beginning to give up hope. He then decided to refer me to Broughton Hall Day Hospital.

**How**

Things are whizzing racing by
There one minute, gone the next
I want to get off – I can't stop the train
For I fear I don't want to go this way again.

Comforting sounds of the music I hear
Out in the sunshine is all that I see
Escape, yes it is, so there I must go,
To flee from the heartaches around me I feel.

The pace is mounting
The fear is getting great,
Where is the gateway
I cannot wait.

Escape, yes I know but I can't hang on
Words, actions, things to do
Where and what I know
Yet how?

Attending a day hospital was difficult because people would ask what sort of work you were doing, or if you were studying, and responding was a juggling act. For a year, I am not sure what I told people. I tried not to interact with people, other than the patients I saw each day at the hospital. My friends, and other normal people, were in a different world, and to reach them was impossible.

**A Touch in the Darkness**

Have you ever felt in the depths of despair
And someone held out his hand.
The warmth, the love and peace that it gave
Acceptance of all that you felt…

For all the words that one could say
Accepting and loving too,
Could do naught to ease the frightening pain
Of someone who's drifting away.

But a hand that holds you,
And says it's okay – the touch that means so much,
Can bring back life and hope
When sometimes all seems lost.

I was admitted to the day hospital on 2 June 1964. There was a very full program each day for eight hours. It consisted of a morning meeting at 9.30 a.m. that every patient was required to attend. Patients and staff would sit in a big circle. All the staff had to be there: doctors, nurses, occupational therapists, social workers and the psychiatrists, who ran the meeting.

The day hospital was a big building with offices on the ground floor, in the centre of which were stairs. They wove their way in a circular shape, bending and swaying till arriving at the mezzanine level where the treatment rooms sat. Carpeted stairs led to the cold, sterile, treatment rooms used for insulin and ECT treatment. You would not go up there unless you were having treatment. On the ground floor, in a big open area as you entered the building, was a meeting room, and it was there that the morning meeting was held every day. Other smaller meetings were held there at various times. They were organised by members of staff for a variety of needs. It was probably where they held the meetings with relatives. They were arranged to enable the staff to meet the patient's family in order to assist in the treatment process.

Morning meeting started promptly. There was silence at first. Not a voice to be heard. It was as if staff were waiting until someone was driven to their absolute breaking point because of the silence. Eventually, one by one, patients would talk about how they were feeling and staff would respond. Staff would be taking note of how their particular patients were that morning. The meetings were tense; there was often crying or anger at staff for various reasons.

Then there were the small groups, relaxation, occupational therapy, art, games, socialisation groups, and many appointments with the psychiatrist and social worker and other members of the treatment team, as required for the particular patient. Most patients were on medication, some more than others. ECT was given for some as well as insulin therapy, and many had psychotherapy with a psychologist or psychiatrist. LSD was still given to certain patients at that time.

I found it very difficult to attend the groups and in fact didn't attend on many occasions. Instead, I wandered around the gardens, becoming more and more anxious. For that reason, I was regarded as a difficult patient. It was very hard for me to attend due to my anxiety, which made me fearful. It became an enormous difficulty for me to walk into a room to attend a particular group, as it felt very threatening. Severe anxiety and panic attacks were not very well understood in those days and many people were misdiagnosed. It was not until much later that they were recognised as specific illnesses, and treatments were altered in the light of increased knowledge.

The memories of that period of my life are still very clear but they mostly exist in the form of feelings of hopelessness, despair and loneliness. I felt cut off from the world at the same time as being part of it. Long heavy days dragged my feet from one place to another, one step at a time. The anxiety gripped me, vice-like; at times I felt I could not breathe and could feel my heart beating loudly – should I run?

**Sounds of Silence**

From the silence come whispers of a longing,
A gaze now intent, the expression of a need,
Blending with the silence it permeates the warm
Now aching receptors
Of one attuned to a struggle for survival.

The sounds of silence speak louder,
The vibrations now quiver tremulously
As they clamour anxiously to fill the vacuum,
A word, a question – now it cannot be filled
The aching search continues as silence falls once more.

All around the world continued, oblivious. It is a silent illness. After a while the anxiety became overwhelming and it was hard to keep going. At times I considered suicide, as the pain was so great: surely there must be a release from this, some place, somewhere. Silence was the answer, always the answer.

In every way I missed the beat, coming in at the wrong bar, and at the critical point, hesitating, which was bad for a percussionist. Music flowed, it had a rhythm, a beauty, it gave you hope. Even in its darkness, eventually it would resolve. But music is one thing, living life is another. My life jarred, with its staccato rhythm and restricted flow; a quietness (silence), but not a peace. It may have looked to everybody else that everything was okay, but inside it wasn't. To a visitor a house may look habitable, beautiful even, with everything you would need but who would have known what went on beneath the surface? Life went on, as it does of course, and fortunately for me it did. No one was killed, all survived, if scarred, at least, by the living.

And so depression becomes one's partner as if it too has given up. My shoulders were heavy, my mind slowed and blocked, and I couldn't concentrate – was life really meant to be like this? The world was not helpful, every loud sound caused me to jump, the slightest unexpected movement shot fear through my body, loud voices or sudden change all brought with it fear and eventually despair and my hands were shaking most of the time. It was impossible to look normal.

**Sounds of Darkness**

Sounds of darkness
Pangs of fear
How can I know if you are near?
To reach, yes, and touch,
To feel and to know
The reassurance of a love that cares
Yet to reach you God
Are you there?

In an empty pit so hollow and deep
Surrounded by a numbness that stings
Only love can break the fetters of fear
And dissolve the numbness as it clings.

The whys and ifs I wonder God;
The answers to them can be found
But, how? God? How?
Must I break in two?

Will you stay not awhile
But linger
And scatter the fear-strewn pathways,
With the hope of peace and love?

As I was on reasonably high doses of medication at times, I felt heavy, weighed down and slow. It felt like there was little purpose to life as there was no guarantee that things would ever be different. The doctors, nurses and all the staff were very caring and I believe each one did everything in their power to help us to get well. To my regret I often did not appreciate that; I could barely keep going but I always knew that one day I would write about what I experienced. I will not forget the people who were on my journey with me. But for them, I would not be here today.

The worst and most frightening experience was when I had to go for psychological testing. It was extremely difficult for me and I was very sensitive to the fact that I was unable to perform as a normal person would. What I mean is, I had been teaching, and had completed university and teachers' college and now I was unable to do simple tests. The Rorschach pictures they showed me were terrifying; all I could see was witches, evil black women with thin, hard, cracked faces and piercing black eyes which tried to penetrate my being. They were boring a hole through me, it seemed – they knew what I was thinking, just like my mother. A long, skinny arm, black and spindly, appeared to be snaking its way towards me, and I ran from the room, and kept running.

Things were not good. I was aware of this and I was scared. What of the future? What would happen? How could I get out of this and back to normal? It seemed to be a long road, and there were to be some difficult times ahead. My mother kept telling me that there was nothing wrong with me; I just needed to pull myself together and get a job and I would be all right. I tried to believe her. As a result, I had many jobs, failed to keep them, and felt more and more inadequate.

I was not a good patient, as was often repeated to me; I would not attend groups or the required sessions I was supposed to. I just needed to be on my own; groups only exacerbated my strong feelings of inadequacy. And so I was labelled as uncooperative, which was true. However, I did attend any appointments with my doctors and the social worker who I saw twice weekly.

Miss McCoroskin was a lovely person who helped me enormously and to this day I think of her dedication to her work and how much I owe to her. We spent hours talking about my difficulties at home and in the relationship with my mother. She slowly and patiently helped me to work through these difficult times, given that I was very immature and lacked knowledge in areas which most people were aware of much earlier in their development. I didn't know some basic things about life and certainly did not have models of how life was supposed to be. The doctors, nurses and the social worker helped to educate me about life in so many ways and were encouraging and supportive of me.

I had tried to be myself, to forge my own identity but I was hindered by the fact that my mother had fixed ideas about who I should be, how I should act, dress, speak, be a friend – about everything, in fact – and I never measured up. To go against her would be to cause enormous problems and of course that is what had to, and did eventually, happen. Most of the time I felt hopeless, anxious, fearful of the future and lacking in confidence in myself. In fact, I no longer knew who I was.

**Breaking**

The pain of heartache, fragments of life

Just piece by piece they disperse.
Peace, like the stillness of night,
No echo of reality to mar this time
Wind comes up and gently stirs the air,
Awake in a world, alive, in touch,

On wings of love, a dream to follow.

Wherein lies for a moment, union, a touch, warmth, life.
To discard it, a wish, but too soon –
Life laughter, an abundance of joy,
A purpose to be accomplished…
A time to die…

On 2 September 1964, Dr Barnes wrote a letter to the Education Department accompanied by a medical certificate – one of many – stating that I would be able to return to work in two to three months' time. Another letter, written on 18 December 1964, states that since I was making steady progress at that time it was believed that I would be fit to be discharged in six weeks' time. The plan, the letter stated, was for me to return to Blackfriars for four days each week and to attend the day hospital on the remaining day so that my response to the work situation could be assessed and a more accurate prognosis arrived at.

The doctors decided also that I needed to learn to become more independent and to that end Dr Metcalfe arranged for me to go to the night hospital, which was in the grounds of Rozelle Hospital, in the same complex. I quite enjoyed being there and being independent. From there I was to go to work at Blackfriars once more.

I began work again at Blackfriars in February 1965 after a long break. I continued to attend the day hospital one day a week until July of that year. Although the staff were wonderful and supported me in every way possible, it was apparent to the hospital staff, the teacher in charge at work and myself that this could not continue. I would sit at my desk and while I was working, marking books and occupied, for a time it went well. And then I would stare out the window and become lost in a dream of somewhere else, and then panic would take hold of me, forcing me to run so as to escape the cloak of fear I was enveloped by. It was not only me that was unhappy; I was causing havoc wherever I was. It was a most unsatisfactory situation. I cannot imagine this occurring today. Besides, today there would be much less support than I received at the time. I was fortunate.

On 11 August 1965, I was readmitted to the day hospital on a full-time basis. After a short time, during which it was apparent that I was not getting better, Dr Barnes, in a letter to the Education Department, stated that although I had been attending the hospital, no further progress had been made, and in fact there was evidence of further deterioration and greater disturbance of behaviour. I was given a further six months' leave of absence. Dr Barnes decided that I needed to be admitted to Broughton Hall as an inpatient. At the big gates to the inpatient hospital there was a sign saying 'No Exit'. To me, then, it seemed quite appropriate, as there really is no exit, as in 'no going back', once a person has been admitted to a mental or psychiatric hospital. It leaves a scar not only because of what has occurred, but because of the attitudes of others about it. If you were to tell anyone.

I remember wanting to be there, wanting to be protected, as I was unable to do that for myself, wanting to be safe from the world and its expectations, and to be in a quiet peaceful place where there was some understanding. Increasingly, I had been leaving the day hospital to avoid the morning meetings, and would wander over the road to walk in the beautiful gardens of the inpatient hospital. The staff there were very caring people who tried to do their best for their patients. They were 'concerned' about me, as I later found out through reading my medical file, and for that I will always be grateful.

As I have indicated, my mother was difficult, and there was no way I could get better while under her influence. It was such a struggle; I remember being asked to sign the admission form – that is, to agree to being admitted to hospital. My mother was sitting beside me and I was aware that she did not want me to be admitted, so I refused to sign the form. At that point I was aware that I might have been put on Schedule 2, and admitted involuntarily. Finally I was admitted, after the staff asked my mother if it was all right for me to sign the form and she agreed. Reluctantly.

**Is This the Way?**

The two of me; the one of me,
How could I know which one it might be?
Flowers and gardens, heartache and fear –
Sometimes go away, and then come near.

Joy and love so warm, so free
Sometimes come and surround me –
But there, in the trees,
A darkness and fear:
Please go away and don't come near.

If God could take my life,
With the love He has given.
Show me the way to steady the flow…
Of darkness on one side, oh, so low…
And peace on the other, why must it go

Oh God at times I see the light,
But the pain of darkness
I wish that it might
Give me peace forever
Or help me find the light.

To grope among trees,
find light in the sky
The little bird so beautiful so free,
Is there pain there
For him as for me.

So easy to go, just wander away
Grasping at the beauty that will not die,
The beauty of love and the joy of life
A long rope with two ends
Peace at one, fear at the other…
Oh God ! Could it but break in two.

So, while I wander in the gloom
The straws that I clutch at are but passing –
There one minute gone the next
But love is there forever –
Sometimes it just gets lost.

I was admitted to ward four on 16 August 1965. It was a mixed ward, with both male and female patients. They were very unwell; during the night I was frightened because people were walking around in the darkness and I could sense someone beside me like a shadow, who seemed to be going through my things, perhaps looking for cigarettes. I froze. Sad, lonely, confused people, trying to cope in a world which was unaware of their existence.

I loved the gardens and spent most of my time wandering in the little walks and pathways, crossing the bridges to sit on various seats or under a tree. Close to nature, there is always a perfect peace. These gardens have remained embedded in my memory and I can call them up at will. I read the following in a brochure about Broughton Hall, when I visited in 1995, and was grateful that this doctor had such a vision which undoubtedly has been healing for many patients.

> Dr Sydney Evan Jones was Medical Superintendent at Broughton Hall from 1925 until his death from cancer in 1948. He took a great deal of interest in the welfare of his patients. He believed that the Broughton Hall gardens should be used 'as machinery whereby a patient's mind could be directed from neurosis to normality'. Jones designed and landscaped the gardens around the more established trees and lawns of the old estate. It is reported that he offered continuing free accommodation for convalescent patients who, as skilled but unemployed artisans in the 1920s depression, were to work with him to construct the ponds, bridges, walls, steps and footpaths. 'The Glen', a secluded area with bridges and ponds, has a wide variety of mainly native trees and bamboo. Broughton Hall was a centre of innovative treatments and a major training hospital. A day hospital was established to provide continuing care in the transition to community life, together with an out-patient's clinic.

The Glen was my favourite place; the peace remains for me a treasured remembrance. How could one know how much it would mean to someone whose mind was in turmoil.

With the ECT treatment, I was improving and feeling more hopeful about the future. My doctor had told me I was to have twenty treatments, twice weekly. After the first two or three, I started to feel different, happy even. I felt more like myself. But still I was torn between pleasing my mother, who did not want me to be in a public hospital, and knowing that I had a chance of getting better there.

While I was at Broughton Hall, my mother came to visit me every day. I didn't want her to, not then, because I knew that the staff didn't want me to see her. I felt as if I was in a bind: I told her that I did not like it there as I knew that was what she wanted to hear, but I wanted to stay a while. I didn't want to leave those beautiful gardens where peace reigned. I believed that there I would get better – eventually.

One day, after about four weeks, my mother brought along my uncle when she came to visit me. He had come down to Sydney because his brother, who was a doctor and had seen me while I was in Narrabri, told my uncle that in his opinion I would never be well again. He advised my uncle to get me out of the hospital. My family were all embarrassed that I was in a psychiatric hospital, and especially one in the public health system. And so along they came, to the hospital. The big guns. My uncle, my mother and 'the man in the office'. Not my father. They marched in and demanded that something be done. They complained to the hospital, saying that they did not believe I should be there. They had their reasons. It was a terrible place, my mother said; she would rather see me dead than in there.

And so the powers that be agreed to let me leave but made a note that I was never to be readmitted, having discharged myself against medical advice. Sometimes I wonder, if I had stayed, whether I would have recovered then, as I believe they were able to help me. But it was to be several more years and several more doctors before that was to happen.

I was discharged from Broughton Hall on 9 September 1965. I went back to Narrabri to stay with my aunt and uncle for a few weeks. That was a good place to be. Since I was about nine or ten years of age, I used to spend the August school holidays there. In 1953 I went there by train, accompanied by my teacher Miss Cox, who was also travelling to Moree, where my aunt and uncle were living then. Those were happy times. I didn't ever want to go home. I used to wish my auntie would adopt me.

Uncle Ian taught me to drive when I was fourteen. 'Get in the car,' he said, opening the driver's side door of the Land Rover. He walked round to the passenger side, opened the door and got in. Then he leaned over, grabbed hold of the gearstick and put it into gear. 'Off you go,' he said, picking up his newspaper and settling back to read. He took me to the police station to get my driver's licence when I was old enough.

After my uncle introduced me as his niece, the policeman looked at me and then at him. 'You teach her, did you, Ian? Well, that's good enough for me.' And he handed me my licence. That kind of thing wasn't unusual – years earlier, my auntie obtained her driver's licence for six duck eggs!

She always said that I would marry a farmer. On this trip, I met Warren Eather, a farmer's son and friend of the family. He and I got on very well together and I was beginning to enjoy myself and feel normal again. However, after I had been seeing him for a short time, Warren's parents found out that I had been in a psychiatric hospital and forbade him to see me again. It was a great disappointment for me, as we had both enjoyed being together. I never saw him again and returned to Sydney soon after that.

But I did not improve. The same situation was still there; it lived there at my home of course. With me. From there, I tried working but was highly unsuccessful.

In September Dr Stephen admitted me to Bromalan private hospital as there were no vacancies at Waddell House. Looking back, it is hard to recall what I did all those months in hospital. Not much, I would imagine. What a waste of a life. Most of the time I was on so many drugs that I had little energy to do anything. Hardly anyone except my mother came to see me, so I had no news of what was happening in the outside world. In later life, I was to find it difficult to talk about my life in the conversations which began, 'Wasn't it fun when we were young?'

Mental illness was a taboo subject, especially if you were trying to get a job. Firstly you needed a curriculum vitae. This wasn't a problem as I'd had lots of jobs. It forced me to stretch the truth, though. I hated to do that, preferring to tell the truth, which meant of course I didn't get the job. No one would employ a person who had had a psychiatric illness. Mental illness was the pits.

Being in hospital was being institutionalised. You did everything by the clock, the nurse's routine, the doctor's routine (if they had one – we used to wonder), and it was all a far cry from what I had been used to.

Sometime in 1966 – I can't remember the exact date – I was admitted to St John of God Hospital in Sydney, on two occasions, for a total of four weeks (also to another private hospital on the North Shore). Dr Smartt was my doctor then. I had several of what were called abreaction treatments with intravenous Ritalin. After the Ritalin – a little while after, as I felt very good at first – I felt like climbing up the wall. It was never given to me again because the drug was very addictive. That was the last time that I was in hospital in Sydney.

**Fear of Falling**

Fear of falling, losing grip
Clinging to a fragile thread,
Freedom yes, responsibility too,
Loss of innocence forever,
In search of self, shattered illusions
Discovery of a shadow till now unknown
Blackness, full of unfulfilled desires
Acceptance of self, guilt, fear
A new self, loving –
But destructive. Torn, twisted
By an outward appearance of calm
Inside raging torments of the past
Expectations of self now incongruent
The same past, a new future
A present fraught with struggle
A search for truth – life's journey.

Some of the things which happened to me in one of the private hospitals, I believe should never have happened. It was highly unethical. But I decided not to include them here, as the majority of care I received was very good. And because people make mistakes. To err is human.

## Jobs

My father did my tax returns. He was an accountant. 'It's a nightmare,' he said. 'I've never seen anyone who has had so many jobs.'

My first job was at age fifteen in John Sands, a very busy stationery shop where I worked for six weeks in the Christmas holidays. My father knew someone who got me the job; that was how it was in those days. I earned seven pounds five shillings a week.

From December 1960, and during my years at Sydney University and Sydney Teachers' College, I worked at Farmers for three months during the Christmas season. In about 1965, during which time I was attempting various other jobs, I applied for a job as a nursing assistant in a hospital for alcoholics. I lasted one day. I actually liked that job, I learned to give an injections by practising on an orange. Another was a live-in job at a children's home. I liked it at first, but I lasted only a few weeks.

I had no trouble getting jobs as I could show I'd had plenty of experience,providing they didn't question the dates or how long I had been in those jobs. Keeping them was the problem. As always, my anxiety returned. It crept up on me like a prowling animal, jumping at me out of the blue. Out of nowhere it surrounded and gripped me so tightly that my only option was to flee. Or so I believed.

One of the jobs I feel most disappointed about, looking back, was a housekeeping job for Judge Curlewis. I was to live in and to take care of his three children. It didn't go well. I lasted one day, perhaps less. I could not cope and ran away. I shudder to think of it now, as it must have taken a lot of explaining by someone.

Then there was my attempt to start a nursing career. I had done a pre-nursing course at age eighteen, with a friend, and decided I would like to try nursing proper. Betty Anderson, the matron from Waddell House, came with me. She had continued to support me even while I was in the other hospitals, and to take me to church with her. One Sunday, as we were walking through the subway at Wynyard Station to go to church in the city, she said, quite out of the blue, 'If your mother hurts you any more, so help me God I'll kill her!' That stopped me in my tracks.

After the plane trip to Brisbane, I settled into the nurses' quarters for one night. All night, in a little room, in the nurses' quarters – waiting – till the next day. I could not cope. The anxiety was welling up inside me to the point where it became overwhelming. And so I left yet another job, and I returned to Sydney the next day. If people ask me whether or not I've been to Brisbane, I try to avoid the question, change the subject or say I visited once briefly. My mother came to meet me at the airport and she was very angry that Betty Anderson had gone with me.

Another job I had was as a nursing assistant in a nursing home run by the Central Methodist Mission. I had my own room, which was good. It took me a little while to settle in. Dr Smartt knew I was working there and I thought he would be supportive. However, there must have been some comment made about me or my past; people in the church and at Waddell House certainly knew my history. Just as I was beginning to settle in and enjoy the job, and being in my own place, I was summoned to Matron's office to be told, 'We do not require your services any more.' Apparently Dr Smartt had told the staff that he could not guarantee that I would not steal drugs from the drug trolley and take an overdose. I was angry. I felt betrayed, rejected and defeated.

The matron handed me my pay and I was expected to leave immediately.

I handed my pay envelope back to her. 'You can keep it.'

'You can't do that,' she said, and pressed the envelope back to me.

'Can't I?' I pushed the money across the desk to her again. 'Put it in the offering plate on Sunday.' I was so annoyed. It was not fair, I thought. I found out later that drugs had been disappearing from the medication trolley. How on earth could I get a job?

In the meantime, I needed to return home as I now had nowhere to live. I suppose I was lucky to have a place to go. However, I now had to sleep in the double bed with my mother again as my brother was sleeping in my old room. I was pleased for him. For the first time in his life he had a room to sleep in, a bedroom that is, as opposed to the dining room, the lounge room and the sun room. It must have been very hard for him over the years.

The longest-lasting job I can remember at that time was at the NSW Spastic Centre. I worked there as a volunteer for three months. It was around 1966, I can't recall exactly. It was very rewarding and satisfying. I remember little Peter Lamb, two years old, a dear little boy whom I assisted with his meals. The occupational therapists were very good – it was there that I started to realise that social work was what I really wanted to do, one of the helping professions. But that was still a long way off. First I needed to find a way to normal everyday life and to hold down a job. Therein lay my problem.

A short time after that, I went to work at the Salvation Army Hostel, assisted by a referral from my doctor who was a Salvationist and knew the matron well. The Salvation Army Hostel was in Darlinghurst, just along from Taylor Square on the corner of a busy intersection. I wanted to try living on my own as I had just been discharged from hospital once again. I can't remember exactly the date as there were so many hospitalisations, but it was towards the end of 1966.

I decided to give it a try; there was accommodation included. The matron was lovely. I was given a room, which was very small, a cubicle really, and the walls were made of what seemed like cardboard. If you were to climb up onto the dressing table, you could see into all the other rooms. There was not much privacy. My job was cleaning, and horror of horrors, or so my mother thought, I had to clean toilets and bathrooms, as well as all the rooms of the people living there. There were three of us employed to do this. I loved to polish the big brass knob on the front door of the hostel. It was a fine entrance, and it shone out to the world, I thought, seeming to provide a welcoming presence just by being there. My mother did not approve and refused to tell anyone who inquired where I was working.

The job was great, very easy – mindless work, in fact. But I was employed gainfully, and living on my own, supporting myself, and I felt pleased with my progress. Matron was a warm, middle aged, well-rounded woman, with a motherly look about her. She looked after the three of us. Jenny was very young – only nineteen. Marilyn was older, but younger than me. She had three children and was struggling to make ends meet. At the time, I had started a glory box, as you did in those days, and I had some beautiful things which I had managed to buy while I was teaching, among them a lovely children's tablecloth, snow white in colour with rich blue markings surrounded by yellow ducks, as well as other much-treasured linen. Marilyn was struggling, she needed them more than me, and besides who knew what my future would be? So I gave them to her.

Every morning after breakfast we had prayers in the dining room, after which we went upstairs to start our cleaning. We had to clean all of the rooms, polish the silver and brassware and generally sweep up. One day, someone broke into Matron's room and stole many of her valuable possessions. It would have been easy, given the walls did not go up to the ceiling. And in a Salvation Army hostel you would trust people, or at least we did. We three girls were all called down to the dining room to talk with Matron. Marilyn, with the three children, had been working at the hostel for a while, and then there was Jenny. Young Jenny. Now, Jenny had been under Matron's wing for several years, having come from a deprived background. She was nurtured by matron and was her pride and joy.

Matron addressed Marilyn first. 'Did you steal the things from my room?'

Marilyn said, 'No.'

Then she turned to young Jenny. 'Did you steal the things from my room?'

'No,' said Jenny.

Then she turned to me and asked the same question.

I was shocked. I could not believe this was happening. 'No, of course not,' I told her.

Matron paused for a moment. She looked at the other two girls, and then turned to me. 'I'm sorry, you'll have to go. You see, Jenny has been here a long time, and she says she didn't do it, and Marilyn has also denied it.' I was the most recent arrival, a patient discharged from a psychiatric hospital – which Matron knew – so I was the one who had to leave.

Taking my pay, I thanked Matron, and with tears in my eyes I gave her a hug and said, 'I didn't do it, Matron, and furthermore, I know that you know I didn't do it.' She smiled, and I thanked her again. I waved goodbye.

Sadly, I took my leave from the hostel, through the door with the shining brass knocker, down the steps, along a footpath, then onto Taylor Street. It was a job I had so enjoyed. I'd felt safe for the first time in a long while and I was beginning to get back on my feet. I felt a huge sense of loss.

Another setback.

# 5

> I yield to that suggestion
> Whose horrid image doth unfix my hair
> And makes my seated heart knock at my ribs
> Against the use of nature? Present fears
> Are less than horrible imaginings.
>
> Shakespeare, Macbeth

Leaving Sydney for Perth, at the age of twenty-three, was probably the most critical event in my life. I felt a combination of great excitement and sadness, as well as a sense of loss.

It happened like this. On a warm February morning I went to my appointment with Dr Smartt. He worked from an office in 135 Macquarie Street in Sydney. I had walked up the street to the doctor's office many times over the years, from the age of nineteen. And so, with the usual heavy heart, anxiety gripping my body throughout, I negotiated a path through the crowds of busy people, on their way to work or to whatever gainful or non-gainful pursuit it might be. Whatever it was, it was a far cry from my space in life. I went through the entrance with the heavy ornate doors, made from heavily reinforced metal and glass, and up to the eighth floor. I pushed the button to go into the secretary's room then went over to my seat, in my usual spot in the corner, alongside a small window, through which the warmth of the sun touched my skin with its comforting presence. My heart was heavy, my mind was racing and there was a knot in the pit of my stomach. I waited.

Once inside the surgery, a feeling of apprehension enfolded me. The doctor was seated behind his big wooden desk as usual. There was a couch against the wall opposite, and one or two chairs sat facing the desk. It was the standard office of Macquarie Street specialists, nestled within dingy, cold and time-worn buildings with slate floors. There must have been many patients like me who had come here over the years.

Rock'n'roll music was popular at the time I began to be treated for anxiety and depression: it accompanied all my moods and it pinpoints for me now the desperate feelings of that time, so that entire feelings flood back on hearing a few bars of Johnny O'Keefe's 'Come on and take my hand', or Buddy Holly's 'Rave On', along with 'The Ballad of Lover's Hill', 'Little Arrows' and 'Saved by the Bell'. This music triggered feelings of panic within me, followed by a feeling of spiralling downwards, a sense of hopelessness and a sense of the futility of my life. Despite that, I kept playing them, because it also provided comfort. I still have some of those records, only a small bundle, though, because my mother smashed a pile of them to prevent me playing them over and over again.

And so, on this particular doctor's visit, he had not much to say. It was a case of 'Well, I don't know what to do with you.'

In my mind, I thought, 'Four years, many long months of hospitalisation, loaded up with drugs and still the hopelessness continues.'

Finally he said, 'The best thing you can do is to get as far away from your mother as possible, preferably London, and if not London then Perth…otherwise you'll never be well.'

I was stunned. I understood in that moment that he was right. Those words marked the beginning of a totally new life.

I felt upset and confused. With the words ringing in my ears, I left the surgery and went straight to the nearest Ansett Airlines office and bought a ticket to Perth. With my handbag in my hand, I headed for the airport lounge to get on the next plane.

Once there, I presented my ticket to the lady at the counter. 'I wonder if it would be better if I went home to pack some clothes.'

'I think that would be a good idea,' she said.

I changed my flight to two days later, went home and announced to my parents that I was off to Perth. My father was devastated. I'll never forget that moment – the look on his face. My mother? I don't really remember. Whatever she said, I had made up my mind. Years later she said that by leaving I had denied her the grandchildren. After I packed some clothes and a few things in my bag, my mother drove me to the airport and said goodbye. I was excited, perhaps a little anxious, but I was looking forward to a new life.

The first thing I remember after stepping off the plane in Perth was the heat. As I walked across the tarmac, the full force of it hit me. I had never felt heat like it. Having spent so much time in Narrabri and Moree in my childhood, I remember the weather being very hot. But this was different. I felt a shiver of pleasure at the thought that I was on my own and could do what I liked, plan my own life. No one would know where I was at any time. I liked that.

In Perth there were only two people I knew, and I had already contacted them both before I left Sydney. One friend who was working for Lifeline in Sydney kindly rang her parents and I was fortunate enough to stay with her for a short while. The first night, I stayed at the Salvation Army Hotel called the Railton. It was all very exciting. The next day, I went to see the mother of the other friend I knew from Moree. He was working in Katanning in the south-west of WA. All was going well; I had hopes that I could start a new life where no one knew my past. How wrong I was.

After a week or so, I made enquiries at the youth hostel in West Perth, and soon after moved in, sharing a room with three other girls a little younger than I was. It was enjoyable, we had a good time together and I was living normally, with other people close to my own age.

Having been retired from teaching on medical grounds, I had thought quite a bit about what I wanted to do. After working at the Spastic Centre and in children's homes and being involved with young people as a teacher, I came to the decision that I would like to become a social worker. I had even made enquiries at Sydney University about their Social Work degree but found that it was highly academic with little or no practical experience involved – not exactly what I wanted. When I arrived in Perth, there was a social work course beginning in a couple of weeks, the first one to be offered in Perth. Social work was relatively new in Australia at that time. This was a small group of twenty people. The course was to be held at WAIT, the West Australian Institute of Technology, and so it had a practical base. I was really looking forward to it – it all sounded too good to be true. I was required to attend an interview in Wellington Street before enrolling; this, I thought, was merely a formality, as I knew that I would be eligible.

It was a very hot day and I remember the contrast as I walked down the street and then felt the cold of the air conditioning when I entered the building. In Sydney there was no need for air conditioning. As I'd expected, I found myself in a room, with a man on the other side of a desk, pen poised to make notes about my suitability for social work.

And then it came, the question – there was no surprise there. 'And what were you doing before coming to Perth? Where were you working, and for how long?'

I had to stretch the truth – that is, the length of time I had worked at these jobs. From previous experience, I had learned that. As I had done previously, I tried to talk around the fact that I had started teaching but found I wanted to take a break to try other things, such as working at the Spastic Centre, apple picking, cleaning, weighing up confectionery. And so on.

This interview was important to me and I wanted it to go well. I had had so many rejections. But I sensed he knew that I was leaving something out so I told him that I had retired from teaching. He was quite astute. Given my age, he knew.

Looking straight at me, he said, 'I used to work in the Education Department and I know that if a teacher as young as you has been retired it would have to be on medical grounds.'

I begged him to accept that I was well now and really keen to do the course. He would not listen; the fact that I had been in a psychiatric hospital and retired from teaching, that was it, end of interview. He stood up, leaving me there, my hopes dashed. My life felt suspended in the air.

Unfortunately I started to feel the anxiety again, the panic attacks and the fear and loneliness of being different. Who would understand? There was no one to talk to, as you never divulged a past like mine to anyone. Ever. And it was to be over twenty years before I told anyone about the past.

**Morning**

Like the softness of morning sunshine
The warmth and glow that it leaves
Or the fragrance of a soft rose
The beauty of love is a garden
Full of such wonders to behold.

As the warmth leaves the sun and a wind starts to rage,
The peace that was here is disturbed.
Into a gale and then a storm, and the roses are torn by its power.
Thunder and lightning follow and then
The shaking and quivering of flowers
and trees as they bend and break with the force

The morning returns with the softness of the sun,
Remains of the storm can be seen
Torn branches strewn about, roses shaken by the wind
Soon peace is restored, as the warmth
of the sun spreads over the garden again.

It must have been when I was about eight that I first started to understand the unfairness of life. Actually, I am quite glad that it was early in life because it was a fact to be dealt with, though I did kick and struggle against it.

And so it was that, reluctantly, I made the decision to contact the doctor to whom I had been referred by my psychiatrist in Sydney. I felt there was no hope, it was too hard and at this point I did not feel confident to apply for jobs. This experience had set me back. It seemed to me that if I had been in gaol I would be given a chance – though in both situations you are treated afterwards as if you have to prove yourself in society. In both situations there is judgement. All the old feelings had returned and the hopes for my future disappeared in front of me.

When I arrived in Perth in 1967, Dr Fred Bell was the psychiatrist in charge at Selby Community Day Hospital in Shenton Park. It was run by Mental Health Services WA. And so, feeling lonely, and extremely anxious and with a letter from my psychiatrist in Sydney in my hand, I went along to the to the hospital. Dr Castledine was my psychiatrist at first; it was he who decided that I needed to be admitted. Later, when Dr Casteldine transferred to another hospital, I was fortunate enough to have Dr Bell as my psychiatrist.

Dr Castledine decided that I needed to be given another two months of insulin treatment. Every day, after the morning meeting, I walked down the corridor to the treatment rooms below and would return later to the dining room for lunch. Steps led down to the treatment rooms, which were like little cubicles or prison cells, with just a bed and a chair in the room. It was a different atmosphere entirely to a prison, though; these were rooms for giving treatment to people who were unwell, rather than punishment for wrongdoing. The walls were white and there was lino on the floors. The wooden steps curved round in a spiral leading down to the lower floor. It was quiet, peaceful almost, a place of healing, perhaps, where hope was waiting.

Glass doors fronted the entrance to Selby, which was a short walk from Shenton Park railway station. On entering, you were faced with a long stark corridor which opened out to a big spacious room. Further on were the cafeteria and the offices, which were nestled away in a corner. The big open area was common in day hospitals like Selby; it was used for the morning meetings, various committee meetings and for social events.

Attendance at the morning meeting was a requirement for all patients. There were no exceptions to this; it was part of the treatment. Patients and staff sat around in a big circle. We waited as everyone settled in for the beginning. For some, this may have been more that they could bear; just living was difficult enough. But this was one of the reasons for the meeting each morning: to give an opportunity for patients to share and to talk about their concerns. It also allowed the staff to find out whether there was anything new that had occurred overnight. Day hospitals were a new form of treatment in Sydney and in Perth in the sixties, and the morning meeting was an integral part of it. However, day hospitals did not continue as a preferred form of treatment, as it was found that it was not the most effective treatment for psychotic patients – and perhaps they were not cost-effective.

The cafeteria, or dining room, was a big room where tables and chairs were set up for the midday meal. There was a counter, or servery, and the kitchen was behind that. There you collected a tray, and then lined up to get your meal. Meals were not cooked there, they were cooked in bulk at one of the major hospitals and the food was sent to the various suburban hospitals.

I can still smell the baked apples and custard, a dessert which was very popular at Selby. Needless to say, I have very rarely cooked that dessert since, and if I do, I remember it all again and the memories come flooding back. Later in my life, someone close to me was suffering from depression and needed to be hospitalised. I visited them, but it was very difficult for me; the memories floated back to me along with the strident aroma of baked apples dressed with custard. I happened to be there at lunchtime. Patients were sitting around the tables, chatting about their treatments and their medications. When each person had finished their meal, they got up, took their empty plate to the designated area, scraped the scraps into the bin, and then, if they were on the roster for that day, they would wash the dishes or stack them in the dishwasher. The camaraderie of patients swapping symptoms and treatment details was overwhelmingly brought back to me. I felt that I could not breathe.

There is a certain feeling of comfort, of familiarity, in the hospital situation, and, if you become too used to it, you may not want to leave. That is institutionalisation. After a while, people can become lost to their friends. I had to get out of there. The atmosphere was at once claustrophobic and secure all in one; a place in which you could be caught and trapped if you became too comfortable. This is a feeling understood only by patients of these institutions. Walled off from the world and excised from it due to stigma, it was a haven, a safe place, though one filled with abnormal conversations and behaviours, talk of travel concessions and sickness allowance, boxes and bottles of medication.

Morning meetings at Selby Day Hospital started at 9.30. We sat around in a circle, patients interspersed with the top brass: psychologists, nurses, occupational therapists, social workers, psychiatrists and the jovial guys in charge of netball, tennis, gym and the other recreational activities. Silence reigned as the psychiatrists waited for someone to speak. A shuffling of feet, coughing, the sounds of birds from outside the window. If you arrived late and had to walk across the room to find a seat, everyone would be looking at you. It was intimidating. We waited… I wonder if psychiatrists were aware of the tension building up. It did, whether they'd planned it or not. The tension was unreal, and eventually someone would break down, get angry and start sobbing. Sometimes patients would become more anxious in response to what someone had said. We were broken, hurting people, spilling out our hurts, anger or perplexity, and it all happened in a nicely formed circle.

Sometimes one of the staff would ask one of the patients how they were feeling. Many people were in their own world; it was hard to observe the very palpable pain and suffering, particularly that of patients with a psychotic illness. It was devastating to see how ill they were, what a poor quality of life they had, and how deprived they were of the normal enjoyments of life.

Time would drag interminably and it dragged along with it a heaviness, a load of cares, which it seemed were destined to hang around however much one tried to be rid of them. They clung to you like they felt they belonged, needing to attach; the will to shake them off was in vain. Their heaviness sometimes became a load and it required more than willpower to shoulder it. But where or from whom can one find or tap into a human understanding of a deep sense of failure, of hopelessness, of trying so hard and continuing to fail and 'not quite measuring up'? It was nearly impossible, one felt, to become normal and to interact in society outside the safe and protective walls of the hospital.

It did provide a haven of protection, a place to be, to exist, and the hope that you would get better, with the treatment, support and encouragement from the staff. And of course this happened, and when it did it we were pleased. But there were relapses; this was the nature of the illness, and once again with heavy heart one would resolve to try again, with the encouragement and huge input from the professional staff. They were dedicated people who were committed to doing the very best for their patients, I believe. Many people I have spoken to dispute this. However, I think that they suffered along with us every heartache, and felt our despair when, after months of work, symptoms were still persisting and proving difficult to manage. I remember the love and support which was given me, and it was love, for who would choose to hang in with a bunch of mentally ill patients for the long haul?

Dr Bell did. He never gave up hope for me.

Boxes of chocolates and presents used to be given to nurses on the wards of general hospitals, when the patients got better, were cured and grateful for it. There were always chocolates. I know it, because when I started work as a social worker I could not get over the chocolates and gifts that were regularly given to the doctors and nurses. Alas, in a psychiatric hospital it was different.

Later, in my role as a social worker at Bentley Clinic, attending the weekly team meeting, it seemed that not much had changed in thirty years. The meeting began at 9.30, there was the customary circle of chairs, and the psychiatrist had a big stack of files beside him. The similarities to the old meetings at Selby, with staff and patients sitting together, brought back the old fear and anxiety. Briefly. Things had changed, of course. For one thing, I was now a member of staff, and so I was seeing things from the other side. There were other big changes to the mental health system, too. For example, there were no day hospitals like Selby any more: it was outpatient clinic or inpatient hospital treatment only. And many of the old-style nineteenth-century asylums had been scaled back or even closed down.

Most of the patients at Selby had a psychotic illness, as I have mentioned, and so it was a painful existence for them. Sadly I knew and had friendships with several people who later committed suicide.

There were a few patients at the day hospital who were younger than me, one only fifteen and another about eighteen. It was sad to see young people who were so disturbed. As well as this, there were mothers who at times brought their children to the hospital as they had no one else to look after them. Such young children, with a mother with a severe mental illness – it must have been so heartbreaking for both parents and the children.

It was a sad time. So many people were so sick. We walked around slowly. There really wasn't much to look forward to; just living out each day was hard enough. This was made even worse because the drugs that most of us took caused us to feel very lethargic, such that it was an effort to join in the activities that were expected. You know the ones, the usual occupational therapy – netball and tennis, knitting, making baskets, and other crafts. Activities were held in the afternoons.

And there was a routine: every day had its pattern, its rhythm, its predictability. All the while you were aware that you were away from, and, in a sense, protected from society, the 'real' world.

At the end of the day, we would get on the train to return home or to our place of dwelling, showing the concession passes which came along with the sickness benefits, our heads hanging low with the heaviness of existence. We looked different, I am sure, walking slowly to the station, no spark of life to speak of. It is not easy to get out of this bind even if you really try. For a start, you have a history, you have no job references, you are not – well, I am saying it – 'normal'. Normal people in those days went to work, had a life, went out to parties and movies, laughed and enjoyed their life. Or most young people did. In that sense, everyone hopes to have a life which is normal. Normal life has its problems too, of course. But at least you are accepted and you can join in the conversation of life.

It was a waiting game, really. Even if you spent a year in hospital, the time passed just the same, and when you looked back you saw a year dotted with appointments with the psychiatrist or social worker, or treatment of one type or another. There were these appointments and then there was yoga and relaxation exercises. They were not helpful at all, for me. There was no way in the world I could ever relax. I shook and trembled with anxiety most of the time, and the expectation that I should 'relax' caused me even more anxiety. All it did was to make me feel even more inadequate than I already did. In later years, after I became a social worker, it was recommended that patients suffering from anxiety should not attend relaxation classes.

In the afternoons, if we could get away with it, we spent the time in the den playing the records of the day – rock'n'roll, and all the sixties favourites. They just served to make me sadder, as music triggers off all sorts of feelings in us all. But I enjoyed it; it was time out from the program.

The staff went on about their business drawing up timetables, holding meetings and groups, and arranging social activities. I would hear them while having morning tea, laughing heartily and joking with each other, sharing the weekend's doings with their mates. Within my being, I felt a cry of anguish. Did they realise that in the next room, or right next to them, there lurked the hopelessness which formed the web of my life, which hung lifelessly about me and the other patients, while they 'danced and sang'? It was intensely painful.

In my school holidays, I used to play a lot of tennis. I was quite good and really enjoyed it. However, I didn't keep it up, much to my disappointment. I think a lot of the reason I didn't was because when I was so sick I tried to play but floundered and was unable to hit a ball. There were tennis courts at Selby, but I felt that people were laughing at me when I played because I was so hopeless. No one would believe I had played before, and certainly not that I had been good at it. In fact, I felt that I was good at nothing and for nothing. I disliked going to most the OT activities but never went to sewing, knitting, handicraft, woodwork – anything to do with my hands. I was hopeless and had been told so for many years. I already felt hopelessly inadequate and to be shown up in front of others was just too much. Maybe others felt the same.

The air hung heavily in the corridors of the clinic. We were alert to a need to be alongside each other. We cared for each other – we didn't need words, we just 'knew'. Many hours we spent alone or together, suffering the same depression or anxiety. At times in the contemplation of our lives, psychosis would possess our thoughts and darken them to be no longer recognisable as our own. Attuned to each tiny change or interruption in the behaviour or communication of fellow patients, we sat quietly, beside each other.

I sometimes wonder what long-term effects insulin treatment has on a person – as well as the effects of the intravenous treatments of pentothal, Methedrine and Ritalin that I was given. The controlled administration of intravenous hypnotic medications was called narcoanalysis, and was used in psychiatry in the sixties to provide symptom relief as well as to facilitate bringing forth childhood and other previously withheld traumatic events. Sodium Pentothal was used in order to remove inhibitions, Ritalin as an antidepressant. Indeed, they did bring about a feeling of relaxation and well-being and would have been addictive if continued, I realised. At that time I was taking at least 80 milligrams of valium a day along with other drugs to control my anxiety and the panic attacks. They were not a cure for anxiety and depression, they merely assisted in the process.

**A Reason**

If I knew God had no purpose
when He put me on this earth,
If I knew there was no reason
to bear the pain and hurt.

Then the beauty of His love untold
And the peace He tells us of
The rich green of the grass and trees
The deep blue of the sky.

Such perfection, such peace,
Untouched by man's mistakes
Then I'd let go and leave this life.
A job to do? Oh yes there is

I know for sure it's true
And God I guess He knows
what's best
For me and for you.

Dr Bell recommended that I ask my father to come over to Perth to live so that I could spend some more time with him and get to know him. He said that I needed to develop a relationship with my father, as it would play a big part in my recovery.

My father came to Perth in 1967, applied for a temporary job as an accountant at Wigmores, and stayed with me for two months. Then he returned to Sydney. He came back again the next year and was given a job at the same insurance company for which he was working in Sydney. He lived with me in a flat for a year and we had a wonderful time together. I was able to get to know my father for the first time. We both returned to Sydney at the end of that year.

Over the many years that followed, my father remained the most significant person in my life in many ways. He was a rock. As I have said, my doctor never gave up hope for me – though at one point he nearly did. This was at a low point, after which I had taken an overdose of tablets. I did not want to go on. I took a handful of my father's tablets and a mixture of my own.

**Poem**

All around life goes on with a purpose it seems,
But for one who is caught in a current so strong,
That it rips and tears at the core of one's being,
To love, such beauty that it cannot be held
Just a moment then the pain that it leaves…

I feel too much…I cannot go on…perhaps not for me
God loves so much, so why
The ache for such love, too painful I feel
The answer must lie elsewhere

I was very fortunate to survive. The doctors at Royal Perth Hospital told my father that I had a 50:50 chance of survival. My father told me later that he was heartbroken. He sat up at the hospital all night hoping that I would survive. The staff said to him, 'It's not your daughter we feel sorry for, it's you.' I made the situation all the more unbearable for my father by being very angry when I woke up that I was in fact still alive. And my clothes had all been cut off. I am deeply sorry now for the anguish I caused my father.

By the time I had taken the overdose and was admitted to Royal Perth, all the doctors had given up hope, I think. They were about to send me to who knows where? Possibly Heathcote Psychiatric Hospital.

But Dr Bell said, so he later told me, 'I will get her better. Send her back to me.' He told me he had a difficult time persuading the doctors to agree. I owe my life to him. He told me some time later that he had taken a huge risk, but it paid off. He always believed in me, even when I was unable to believe in myself. He never gave up hope. When he was the director of Mental Health Services, he still continued to see me and support me. He did everything he could for me. I will always be grateful to him and to the many wonderful mental health staff who helped me over many years.

Dr Bell's advice and support has continued to sustain me over many years, and has proved useful in my later work in counselling clients with anxiety and depression. I would often quote the advice that he had given to me and his encouraging words. Of course, I never gave any indication of what I had been through. Several of my clients came back to me and said how helpful it had been and how they had passed this advice on to others who had really benefited from it as well. What an influence he has had on so many lives!

I did recover, but I needed motivation, some determination. Just as my doctor was probably wondering what to do with me, I thought to myself, 'This is it. I'm determined to get better.' I went off all my medications, the whole lot, with no ill effects at all. And I was on my way...

After being at the day hospital for quite some months, I thought that I might try nursing again. It was the helping professions that I was interested in. At that stage, the staff were encouraging me to try enrolled nursing at Shenton Park Rehabilitation Hospital. It was more to have some experience working, rather than to get paid. However, once again, an interview was required. It was to be with the matron, I think, or maybe it was later that she became matron. Anyway, she knew that I had been attending the day hospital and was prepared to give me a chance.

Naturally, in the process of the interview, she asked my name. Silence. Would you believe it, the night I was admitted to RPH after taking an overdose of tablets, she was the registered nurse who was on duty! I found this out later. I was very disappointed as I was desperate to make a start, to work again.

Unless people have experienced mental illness or something similar – the utter despair of ever being well again, the severe feelings of anxiety which dog one's every move, the inability to work or to be regarded as a normal person or to engage in the simple pleasures of life without fear and panic – they cannot imagine how crippling it can be. To have a life which is not real because no one knows you are living it, to live a double life – hospitalisation during the week and trying to be normal at the weekends – is very difficult, especially if you don't know what normal is and you sure aren't acting normal. How on earth can you get back to work if you aren't given a chance?

Perhaps fifteen or twenty years later, I was participating in a Christian meditation course and I noticed an older lady who was sitting a few feet away from me. She looked familiar. And then, I remembered. She was the director of nursing of Royal Perth Hospital, where I had been admitted after taking an overdose. I spoke with her later but she did not know who I was and I did not tell her. By then I was a social worker at a hospital in Perth.

Around this time, my doctor told me that he had written me up in the medical journals, as I was his greatest success. He told me that I was the worst psycho-neurotic patient that he had ever had.

To which I replied, 'Well, thanks very much.'

He rephrased it. 'I mean that you were the sickest patient I have ever had, but the one who has given me the greatest satisfaction because you recovered.' He never gave up hope for me, he believed in me even when I could not believe in myself. He told me, 'I will get you better.'

# Part Three

# 6

> There is a time for everything
> and a season for every activity under the sun.
> Ecclesiastes 3:1

At the end of 1968, my father and I returned to Sydney. Initially I went back home and began to look for accommodation and a job. I was fortunate to find a house in Bondi with four other girls and, at times, their boyfriends. And so I moved in to 11a Ewell Street, where I lived for twelve months, and was very happy there. The next thing was to get a job. I decided to walk the streets and this time to tell people my past history and offer to work voluntarily if someone would give me a chance. I can't remember the places I went to, except that they were in the surrounding area.

And then I came upon Waverley College. It was a Christian Brothers college. I just walked in, asked to see the principal, and explained my situation. I told him the truth, thinking that maybe he would give me a chance.

Brother Simmons listened as I spoke to him. Then he got up from his seat and said, 'Just wait here a moment and I'll speak to the bursar.' He came back a few minutes later and said, 'How about we pay you thirty dollars a week? We'd be happy to have you.'

They would not hear of me working for nothing. The Brothers were kind and caring men. They had agreed to give me a chance and I would not disappoint them. I was very happy.

While I worked there, I learned to type, attending a three-month receptionist course – I was never able to type fast but I could type a few letters if required and gradually I became faster. I did a lot of driving around in the car, taking boys here and there, often to St Vincent's Hospital, after they had accidents, which happened frequently while playing football.

One of the saddest things that I had to do was to visit, on a few occasions, a young man who was only a teenager and was dying of cancer. At the entrance to the institution there was a sign: 'Home for the Dying'. I wondered how this made him feel. I talked to him, tried to comfort him. He was aware that he was dying and had accepted it. It had a significant impact on me, as he was only a few years younger than I was. Surely no one should be in a position where they were dying at that young age. But he was and there was nothing I could do to alter it. It changed things for me; it made me realise that life is so precious. So many people I knew and got to know a few years later died as a result of suicide. I wondered whether their deaths could have been prevented. I became aware of the sanctity of life.

Sometimes I and Mrs Deveridge – the lady I worked with – would have lunch with the Brothers, when invited. They lived a simple life and apart from a few holidays now and then, they worked hard and they were dedicated to the boys. After I left, I kept in touch with a few of the brothers for quite some time. They had given me a chance. When I left, I had a reference and went on from there. They even travelled to Perth to visit me after I moved back there to live in 1970. When you are able to work, to be independent and to have somewhere to live, then anything is possible. Maybe even to be accepted for social work!

For that, however, I was to be rejected once again for a different reason this time, due to the fact that the university wanted to enrol students who would be politically active. That was not the type of course I was interested in at that time.

At that time and over the next twelve months, I walked at weekends, often for three hours, around Bondi and Waverley. I went in the City to Surf and thoroughly enjoyed it; walking it was an achievement for me.

At home, we all took turns to cook and I got on very well with the other girls, mostly New Zealanders. Things were going well at Waverley. It was a very happy time for me. I was able to be myself, to dress as I wished, and to live my life as I wanted. And I was working!

Once a week, after I had finished my receptionist course, I would meet my father for dinner in the city. We went to a little restaurant near Park Street where he worked and I used to order curried sausages and rice. How I loved that. For dessert we would both order waffles and ice cream.

From Waverley College, I made a decision to relocate to Perth and was to spend the next forty-four years there. Before I left Sydney, I had applied to a job advertisement to work in medical records at Royal Perth Hospital. I was able to fill in enough details about my past work; I had had enough jobs. It did help that I had worked at Waverley College for a year and that I had a glowing reference from the principal. No one was to know how I had obtained the job – that I had been fortunate enough to be given a chance, that I was paid thirty dollars per week when the current rate was probably about seventy dollars. That did not matter. To supplement my income, I had worked at the weekends as a kitchen hand in a nursing home.

When I arrived back in Perth at the beginning of 1970, I went to Royal Perth Hospital for my interview, which had been arranged before I left Sydney. It was a bit confronting. However, I was confident and believed that I could do this job. There was a panel of three persons seated behind a desk asking questions of me in turn, and I was able to respond successfully. RPH gave me the job!

So now I was earning a good salary and was able to save at last. My weekly pay was seventy dollars, which was very good at that time. Rent for a one-bedroom flat was eighteen dollars. My housekeeping, a few years later with a small family, was eleven dollars a week, so it would have been less than that.

They were good times. There seemed to be plenty of work available, at least in those jobs for which you did not need qualifications or experience. I remember noticing at the time, when travelling on the train during the day, that the carriages were almost empty, apart from old people and mothers with babies. Was everyone at work? Or was I aware of it because I had moved from Sydney, which was a big city with a lot of people, whereas Perth at the time was more like a big country town in comparison? People who grew up in Perth would later tell me that they had to walk down the back garden to the toilet and some did not have electricity or a washing machine when they were growing up – very different to my experience growing up in Sydney.

Working in medical records was a good job and I enjoyed it; it was a step up from cleaning toilets, although a far cry from teaching or social work, which was my goal. At least I was working in a hospital and that was a start. I was quite well, but still suffered the anxiety and panic attacks at times. I was learning to deal with them, however; I had my ways. Even now I could probably point out to you all the toilets I sat in, shaking, with my heart pounding, trying to calm myself. People never noticed and I managed to pass as normal. I was accepted and got on well with the boss – she even came to my wedding.

One day while retrieving a medical record, I realised that I was very close to where my own medical record was kept, filed alphabetically and sitting in its little pigeonhole, lined up beside the other medical records, only a vowel or consonant away from where I was standing. My heart beat faster. This was my chance. A new beginning. I had a job and I was earning money. I was doing well, I was almost normal.

But this had to be planned. And carefully. I knew it. Stealing medical records…well, who knows? Could I be locked up for it?

I will never forget when I told my psychiatrist, then director of mental health, that I had taken my medical record and destroyed it. It was with a little apprehension that I awaited his reply.

'Good on you!' he said.

Ah, my friend, I thought, or should it be it partner in crime? What a wonderful man.

But back to the undertaking. This had to be planned well; it could not fail. As it happened, my mother was staying with me at the time. She had come over on one of her infrequent visits. In those days, a return ticket from Sydney by plane cost eight hundred and eighty dollars. And remember that my weekly wage was seventy dollars and hers would not have been much more.

Anyway, I explained the plan to her. I needed her to assist me in the process of stealing my medical record, and then to take it home. She was to do the destroying and I was organising the getaway. And so it was all teed up. My mother was to bring her car to the corner of Murray Street, very close to St Mary's Cathedral, and wait there with the engine running. I told her the time I would be there. I was to run out, quickly, in case I was followed. My mother would grab the notes through the car window and take off. I remember my excitement when I phoned her at my flat and she told me she had set fire to my notes in the kitchen sink.

Now I really didn't exist to the world, or at least to the medical records department of Royal Perth Hospital. The main purpose for me was to physically remove the notes which related to my past. If I wanted to revisit that period later in my life, it would be in a different light.

Around 1973 I joined Samaritans, a telephone service for those who are despairing or suicidal. I was there for ten years, doing a weekly shift on a Friday night from 8.30 till 11.30, and an overnight shift once a month on Friday nights. I also worked on New Year's Eve and times when people wanted time off, and they were the busiest times. It was surely the most satisfying thing I have done in my life. I met many lovely people and we all agreed that we got far more out of it than we ever put into it.

It was also a requirement that we were on the emergency squad, which meant we could be called out to see someone. If a Samaritan was on the phone to a person who he or she believed was a suicide risk, the emergency squad volunteer in that area would be rung and asked to go to that person's home to see them. I remember sitting and talking to a man who had some cyanide beside him, and trying to talk him out of it. Another had a bomb. I was not involved with that particular person but after he left our office we learned that a bomb had gone off in Kings Park.

Hope drives away fear and log-like feelings; it embeds in us a seat of sureness, of fixedness, of enduring and we work towards it in our life, in our thoughts and in our actions. To be alone without human touch is to wither, a little each day, to grow weary, to lose expectation, drive and motivation. It is not easy. So sad it is that people can feel so alone and so despairing.

# 7

> True happiness flows from the possession of wisdom and
> virtue and not from the possession of external goods.
> 
> Aristotle

On my third attempt to apply to study social work, I was successful. I studied Social Work at the University of Western Australia from 1986 to 1987.

My first job was at Mt Henry Hospital in Perth in 1988. It was the one I look back on most fondly. It was a big state government hospital. Over three hundred patients with complex medical or psychological problems resided here, and were provided permanent and ongoing care. The hospital was for people who could not be cared for adequately elsewhere. Every effort was made to find a place in the community for them first, but when no place could be found they came to Mt Henry. The hospital had a dementia ward, and a ward for young, disabled people who had suffered a traumatic accident or illness leaving them often with permanent brain damage. While I was there, an excellent palliative care unit was established which was for people transferred from public hospitals who needed care for the last weeks of their lives. Occupational therapists, social workers and physiotherapists provided care and services as needed.

I was responsible for several wards, some with up to thirty people in them. One of them was a ward for people with a mental illness but who were quite independent otherwise. People there had their own rooms, but were provided with meals and other allied health services.

My own aunt was transferred from Sydney to Mt Henry Hospital while I was working there as she had schizophrenia and now her only relatives were here in Perth. Working there was one of the most fulfilling times of my life. I loved my work. I got out of bed each morning grateful that I was able to do this unaided. My role as a social worker was to provide support for the residents, as they were called, and I found I was able to do that because of the experiences I myself had in mental institutions. I knew about living in an institution so I was able to understand, a little better perhaps, how the residents might be feeling. My own experiences of occupational therapy helped me to stand up for those who were happy to be left alone in their room to read books. Some of them would read a pile of library books each week and would talk to me about them, recommending certain ones they thought I should read.

The 'difficult' residents, especially those who expressed anger, and the ones with a mental illness, were always referred to me. It was what I had hoped for; I was able to provide support for people in an area I knew well. Dr Hilda Fleming, with whom I worked, was excellent; she was dedicated to her work and directed the difficult patients to me. We were a good team.

After six years I was seconded to Bentley Clinic, which was under the auspices of Mental Health Services. It was 1996. It was where I wanted to be at that time. I was working in a psychiatric hospital, like the ones I had been in thirty years before. But no one knew. I knew what it was like to be there in hospital, so it was satisfying for me that I could empathise with and also advocate for patients when necessary.

My mother still continued to play her games when I phoned her as I always did over the years.

'Hello, Mum. How are you?'

A short silence, then, 'Who are you?'

'Oh, come on, Mum, you know who I am.'

'Do I know you?'

'It's your daughter.'

'Oh, have I got a daughter? I know I have a son…'

'Come on, Mum, stop it, you know very well who it is.' By now I was starting to feel the familiar frustration, thinking, not again, I'm so tired of this.

Then, 'Oh, I do have a daughter, do I? I'd forgotten all about you.'

'Mum, stop it or I'll hang up.'

It took me years to be able to say the latter and once I did, the game stopped.

There were a lot of young people on the ward. They were very ill, weighed down, sad, lonely, disengaged and losing hope. Especially difficult for me was one client who was the same age as I was when I was admitted. She had been told she was to be given ECT and it had to be discussed with her mother. I felt for her. I had been where she was, years before. I wanted to help her, but I couldn't. I identified with her too much. It was made more difficult for me, I believe, because I was not able to say, 'I have an idea how you feel because…' And I certainly didn't know what to say as a social worker without mentioning that. Because I was a social worker, but I was also that person back then! I didn't know how to be a social worker who hadn't experienced mental illness – that's not who I was. Thus, I was a bit wooden; I couldn't be myself. And soon after that I would decide to get out of psychiatry.

As the young woman's social worker, I went to visit the family. That was going to be very difficult for the family and for the young woman herself. How could I help them? The problem, if I could call it such, was the stigma of mental illness. I had lived with it, having experienced it in many areas of my life, and I had to be so careful not to divulge anything to anyone. And so I lived with the fear of it happening and destroying my life, almost as someone with a criminal past, as I have said previously.

As part of my job, I visited the psychiatric hostels in the area. I ran groups with another social worker to support the relatives of the young people, aged fifteen to twenty, who were suffering from a psychotic illness. The aim was to treat them early, in the hope of a good recovery or prognosis. For my part, I found it satisfying to run the group and to help the relatives of the young people, sometimes suicidal, who were living at home with their families. It was very rewarding, since the group continued to meet long after the original group ended.

In one of the hostels I met again a few of the young women who were in the day hospital with me all those years ago – twenty years later. They had schizophrenia and were now living permanently in a hostel. They still remembered me. Also I learned, sadly, four young people I knew back then had committed suicide. Another of the young men, whom I quite liked, is now in a long-term mental hospital in Perth.

On many occasions I talked with the psychiatrist I worked with, discussing issues, particularly those on which we had a difference of opinion. He was always very interested in my ideas. It was difficult, though, because the reason I had the ideas in the first place was because I had once been a psychiatric patient. Dr Castle was editor of the magazine *Connect*, and he kept asking me to write my ideas in an article for him. I told him I would do so one day. I couldn't do it then.

Working at Bentley Hospital brought back the memories of when I was in Broughton Hall. I wanted to know what had happened to me, and what diagnosis I had been given. And so I decided to go back to Sydney, to Broughton Hall Day Hospital. It was no longer in operation. The building was still part of the mental health system, but by that time was used mostly for administration. I asked to be directed to the medical records department. I was apprehensive, knowing it could be difficult. However, I explained my situation as best I could.

As she handed me my medical file, the medical records officer asked me whether I intended to sue the hospital.

'Of course not, I wouldn't do that,' I said. 'I have nothing but admiration for the mental health profession and I will never forget how much they did for me.'

I paid the thirty dollars and started reading it as soon as I walked away. I was amazed that the diagnosis was what it was, and that the prognosis was 'ominous'. It brought it all back. But I was warned. Dr Bell had strongly advised me not to get the notes for that reason. The memories flooded back to me in big bundles. I could remember being as sick as the medical notes stated; I could remember feeling that it was all too much and that I didn't want to live any more.

Soon after getting the notes, I spoke to a psychologist friend, Laurel, who said, 'It's all in the past, get rid of the notes.'

So, on impulse, I got rid of them. Back to the kitchen sink. Afterwards I regretted it. Fifteen years later, when I was writing my story, I needed them and I had to apply again, through Freedom of Information this time.

When I was a patient at the Broughton Hall Day Hospital, in the late sixties, psychiatrists were not aware of panic disorder. Though it is frequently diagnosed today, it was not recognised as a psychiatric illness until the eighties. In those days, it was known as an anxiety state. I learned from my notes that I had been diagnosed with nervous illness, severe anxiety state, depression, schizophrenia. However, the final diagnosis, made eventually by Dr Bell, was severe and chronic anxiety with panic attacks – a condition made all the more difficult, according to Dr Bell, because it was prolonged and traumatic.

Forever, it seems, I have had the thought that I must write a memoir – quite a common thought or desire when thinking about retirement. It began with a thought here and there, a few scribbles on a page; then, gathering up old poems written in the past; old pages of diaries, journals, notebooks, and scraps of paper. Then I started to sew them together.

There have been a few hiccups along the way, or should I say 'baulkings' at my writing, after some negative comments when I mentioned it to people.

'Just forget it. It was in the past,' was the general advice.

'Why don't you put it all behind you, count your blessings and move on?' I asked myself. Well, I tried that, for forty years. But now, it is as if a part of me has been hidden for years, and I wanted to incorporate that part into the person I am today.

In 2012, I was startled to see a program on *Four Corners* about youth suicide. It was a story about a number of teenagers in a country town in Victoria who had killed themselves by jumping in front of a train. It broke my heart. What can I do? I thought. What can I say that might change things? As much as any personal reasons, it made me realise that I had to write down my story. I'd been in a place where I didn't want to live any more and had come through it to live a meaningful life. So I kept writing. I want people to know that there is hope, there is meaning, and there is purpose in life.

# 8

> When in distress to Him we cried
> He heard our sad complaining;
> O trust in Him what ere betide
> His love is all sustaining.
>
> Henry Baker Williams

My last job was at Osborne Park Hospital in Perth, working in obstetrics. I really loved it; it was one of the best jobs I'd had. It was a normal, general hospital and so a refreshing change from Bentley Clinic. While the women and their families who I dealt with were often suffering from depression and anxiety, some with bipolar disorder or other mental illnesses, that part of the job was interspersed with the day-to-day goings-on of a maternity ward. Seeing so many babies around everyday was a long way from palliative care at Mt Henry! Also, the problems weren't all related to mental health – people also had problems with housing, with relationships, with isolation, and so on. They were things you could help with more easily and it was satisfying to do so. I worked there for eight years.

By 2006, I was looking forward to retirement. One afternoon, my gaze was drawn out the window of my office. It was beautiful out there, the sun resting on the grass warming it for the day, butterflies happily doing their dance. A lawnmower in the distance. Somehow that beauty helped to soften the hardship and despair borne on the backs of the clients of the clinic, who come with a heavy heart hoping for an ease to their suffering. Life can be hard. It can be unfair. No rhyme, no reason, it just is.

**Musing**

A desk, some pencils, books
piled high
A light dispersing some overarching glow
Making nearly sunshine in my
small dark corner.

Frames with children enclosed
Statement of a time passed
Watch over me
Now grown tall, wise and richer.
Fragments of the past attached to their being.

This desk, my life,
small portion now,
Hope fades through the shutters of my
age worn self
Destined to end in a silent peacefulness
As in night fall

With poetry filled
Joy mixed sadness
Embedded in my soul
Breaks out and mutters,
Soon must we depart.

But no, stay a while thus
To scatter the pathways of my being
In small footprints to give thanks
For a life of being
So strident so tall.

Vale

  Knock, knock. The door opens.

The midwife is at the door, holding a referral in her hand. 'Sophie is a quite pregnant young woman. This one has a long history of depression and anxiety. Very little family support, no partner on the scene, nothing for the baby yet – oh, and marital difficulties. Good luck with this one!'

It's Monday morning at the antenatal clinic, and the midwife has brought the first client of the day.

And so the day begins. After finishing with my client, I walk back to the clinic desk to return the medical record and advise the midwife of the outcome. Walking there, I try to negotiate a pathway. The corridor is lined with clients patiently waiting to see the doctor, midwife or social worker. Their children are on the floor, playing with toys on wheels and watching the world continue around them.

Then back to my office. The hospital walls held within them many years' tales of sadness, now piled one on top of another, pages in between, interspersing incidents, and now weighed down with a load of similar packages of grief and distress, all stamped with a medical record number and date of birth. Hurt spilled into my room, mixed with tears, sometimes laughter and relief, wonder, distrust, the gamut of feelings, knocking against each other to find its own saving place.

Walks along the corridor offered a look at the world of the hospital – the best place was the coffee shop, where I would re-energise with a cup of coffee and slice of cake before returning to the fray. Conversations went on around me, from tables on either side – relatives seeking to find some comfort in the distress of the daily visit, some with relief, but all helped by a cup of coffee and a chat.

Between clients there are phone calls, information seeking, distress calls, and the run of the mill administration ones. And so, seven clients later, a look into the maternity ward, and then home.

One of the most amazing and strange coincidences of my life occurred while I was working here. One day, two of my colleagues and I went out for an extended lunch at a local restaurant. We were relaxed; it was a much needed break from a stressful job. As sometimes happens, the talk turned into one of those long conversations about life. Now, I can't remember exactly how the conversation went, just that it got to this: Jacqui was talking to us about her family, and in the course of the conversation she explained that it was actually her father who had brought her up, because her mother suffered from a mental illness and was attending a hospital for treatment when she and her brother were very young.

So far, no problem. All very sad, though. I listened. She went on to say that her mother, whom she called by her Christian name, Hazel, had been at Selby Community Day Hospital; she had bipolar disorder and she was very unwell. She told us that as children they had accompanied her to the hospital on school holidays. She said they disliked having to go there because there were so many sick people.

I caught my breath, I felt my jaw drop. I was speechless.

My colleagues turned to me. 'What?' they said expectantly.

I just sat there. I could hardly believe it. After a minute or so, I collected my thoughts. I needed to explain. But after so many years of silence I needed a moment to think about the risk I was taking.

You see, it was in the sixties when I attended Selby and I knew Hazel. I used to talk to her in the change rooms. I would also talk to her children – two beautiful blonde-haired children aged about two and five. I felt so sad for her and for them as it was obvious to me how very mentally ill she was. I can see them now, those two young children. My social work colleague, Jacqui, you see, was the little girl.

It seemed that my life had come full circle in some ways. I had revisited the hospitals and hostels where I had been, and met some of the people I once knew.

And now…

Selby Day Hospital no longer exists. It was taken over by a community development centre in the seventies. After I left, it went on to run educational programs which were held in people's homes, and currently it is a hospital for geriatric patients, specialising in dementia care. When people insist that there was never a psychiatric hospital on this site, it seems as if we may not have existed. At least in the minds of others, of persons today. But we did, we were there. It is history now; it was a different era. Things have moved on a long way since those times. Most of the patients with a psychotic illness are now cared for in the community, at day centres or live-in hostels and attending daytime activities, or sheltered workshops. Everything changes.

**It will return**

Could it be that the fear that so long was at bay,
Can return with a pang that can sting,
For it holds and gnaws as if to destroy,
The very roots of a life.
Like a beautiful rainbow, a light in the sky,
Is the peace and love one may find
For the love of God as it's promised to us
Can be found when one reaches out –

The love of God it seems to me can be found at the foot of the cross
For in depths of despair, when helplessness and weakness overwhelm
There is the need for a friend to love and to care–
But where is God?
There…yes, right at the foot of the cross.

You always wonder: will it come back again? That bolt from the blue, that anxiety that comes from nowhere, for no apparent reason, and grips you vice-like. But time heals and you are more able to see life as it is. I still take antidepressants and I am the happiest and the most content that I have ever been. I cope with a crisis just as any other person would. But events or situations can trigger things which occurred in the past at times. The medication prevents any adverse reactions to the triggers, coming as they do unexpectedly. Post-traumatic stress is well-known today and someone you know may be affected by it. Traumatic things happen to all of us in our lives and the experience makes us who we are. Grief comes to all of us after the loss of a loved one, and we will all experience sadness, loneliness and emptiness and a range of feelings, depending on the person and the circumstances surrounding the loss, and for some time we may find it impossible to believe that we will ever be happy. But for those around us life goes on and others must continue to enjoy their good times even though someone near to them may be suffering. We can cope. And we need to go on believing that.

Earlier, I talked about the feelings I experienced when I was very depressed and heard the staff at Selby laughing and chattering over their morning tea in the next room. Many years later and with somewhat more insight, I now see things in a different way. We all have a right to enjoy our life, a right to happiness, whatever that may mean to each individual, even though in the world around us there may be sadness and many people may grieve. Of course it is natural and normal for a depressed person to feel annoyed, even angry, when they see people around them laughing and enjoying life while they are embedded in the deepest darkness. However, it would not do for us to descend to the pits alongside them. We should try to be patient and supportive, of course, to a person suffering from depression, but it is very, very difficult to do.

To live with a person who is depressed can be one of the most difficult things to bear. For depression is contagious; it sticks to our skin like a leech, dragging us down along with the sufferer. At first it is a surface feeling then gradually it sinks one's heart deeper into their chest then moves systematically through the body affecting their motivation and mobility, their arms and legs feel leaden and wooden with the heaviness that is gloom. This is depression, which is debilitating and at its worst leads to thoughts of suicide. But we must learn to protect ourselves, to claim our own right to life and to happiness therein, even while someone close to us may be suffering the pain of depression.

I was privileged to learn something from Frances Cooper, who was a patient in the palliative care unit in the hospital I was working in. She suffered from schizophrenia and was in hospital because she was dying from cancer. She had spent time in her life caring for her older sisters, and also bringing up her son, who was now aged twenty-three. On the many occasions that I spoke with her, I wondered why she did not have any visitors apart from her sisters who came when they were able.

She told me, 'I don't expect my friends to visit me. I have told them that they have their lives to lead and they should not come to visit me. I have lived my life and they need to live theirs.' She insisted that she had enjoyed her life. She told me that she used to ride her bike to visit friends and had her own interests, as well as being involved in bringing up her son.

She was an inspiration to me. She appeared to have accepted her life as it was, with all of its hardships, and she did not have expectations of others.

Paper rolled off the printing press before my eyes, the words moving so fast that I could hardly read them. Pages and pages kept coming, bold black words in neat lines on the white pages. Everything I had ever wanted to know flashed before me, page by page, and I was amazed. I wanted to grab the words off the page and hold onto them, but it moved too fast, page after page rolling off the printing press.

I couldn't believe it. Just the day before I was wondering what I should do, what I needed to do. And there it was, right in front of me, all laid out, exactly what I needed to do. It told me all the ways that I should live my life and how to do it. Just like a script. All the answers to questions I had ever wondered were there. As the pages flowed faster and faster off the screen, I was so excited. How could this be? Could I get a pen and write it down? No, there wasn't time. I had to try to remember it all. It was amazing. I wanted to tell everybody, to shout it from the rooftops. I did. At the time I told everyone I could.

And then I woke up! It was a dream. I was shaking with excitement. Being a dream, I couldn't really shout it from the rooftops. And naturally, I couldn't remember all the words and all the advice that was given. I was so disappointed.

But now I knew that there was a way, a path to follow, perhaps I did not need the words, perhaps I just knew? And I could draw on this wisdom when I needed to.

Many quotes and pieces of advice have helped me over the years:

> Don't try to make the cakes that other people make. If you are good at making sponge cakes, then just make sponge cakes. (Nurse Manson, at Selby Community Day Hospital)

> You only need one house to live in and you can only sleep in one bed at a time. And remember, the only important thing in life is relationships. (Dr Fred Bell)

> To thine own self be true, and as the day follows night thou can'st not be false to any man. (Shakespeare, *Hamlet*)

> If things get so bad that you think you cannot go on any longer: hang in there. And hang in there until you cannot hang in any longer, and things will get better. (Dr Lois Achimovich)

> I pray not that thou should'st take them out of the world. (John xvii.15)

> It would be a great deal safer, in one sense, for believers to be taken at once to heaven as soon as they begin to follow Christ. They would then have no temptations, no enemies to fight, no conflicts and struggles to pass through. But who would then do Christ's work in the world? There would be none to tell sinners about the Saviour, none to show to men the beauty of Christ in a holy life, none to witness for God and to fight his battles.
>
> There is another reason why Christians are left here. They are not the most majestic trees in the sheltered valleys, where no storms break, but those rather which are found upon the hill tops and on the mountains, where they must encounter the fierce gales. It is so with men: the noblest are grown amid difficulties and hardships, not in pampered ease. Even Jesus himself was trained in the school of conflict and struggle. It may be the easiest thing to have no battles in life, to grow in some sheltered plain where the storms never blow, to meet no hardships, to have no burdens to carry; but what sort of life comes in the end from such a career? If we would reach the heights of blessedness, we must be content to pass through the fields of struggle. (J. R. Miller, *Come Ye Apart*)

It is perhaps difficult to understand why a person who has faith who is a Christian should want to end their own life. But for me at a time when my life was so fraught with fear and suffering, the only answer seemed to lie in being with God, in heaven. After all, heaven is depicted as a place where there will be no more suffering, where there will be eternal peace, being forever with God. But that is not the way it was intended. Our life is not ours to take and I know now that it is a selfish action, which one will consider only when there seems to be no hope. Fortunately for me, I survived, and how grateful I am. Since then I have learned much more about suicide, counselled many considering it and seen the effect it has on loved ones and friends. For them, it is tragic and inexplicable. It is possibly the worst and most difficult grief to come to terms with, a grief which will never be known to the person who has died.

We know more about the tragedy of it today, and are aware of the importance and necessity of prevention; of making it widely known to the public that help is available. It should be talked about, and people should see it as their responsibility to look out for their fellow human beings, to lend a helping hand, to be compassionate. Mental health professionals especially should be aware that their colleagues may be at risk, as surely this is one of the most draining, the most taxing, bewildering and most dangerous of callings. Psychiatrists are dealing on a daily basis with the quite fragile lives of people who may tentatively reach out for help in a crisis.

Attitudes towards mental health have changed considerably, I think, particularly in the last few years, and people openly talk about it without fear of being judged, in most cases. Mental health professionals, however, seem to feel that they must never show any signs of anxiety or depression and so they often suffer in silence, I believe, and sadly, sometimes end their lives. Possibly it is here that the stigma remains today. Because there is a possibility that disclosure of mental illness may pose a risk to their jobs.

For these reasons, my decision to write of my experience had to be at a time when I had retired or was no longer employed as a health professional. How much help could a person potentially give if he or she were allowed to speak of his or her experience and thereby to give some hope to one who is desperate? Not necessarily to speak openly of the experience but to let a person know of their fellow feeling. We all need hope; lack of hope is the ultimate problem, the reason people are driven to desperate measures. If the stigma were removed, perhaps more people might be prepared to reach out, to reveal their weakness or strength, as it may be, believing that one can recover and even live a 'normal' life.

There is a widespread belief today that too many people who do not need it are taking medication for depression. I acknowledge that this is a problem. However, we may need to exercise caution here, because those who are significantly depressed and in real need of medication may be the very ones who heed the suggestion that there are too many people on medication for depression who do not need it. My real concern here, though, is the attitude of some mental health professionals to taking medication. Mental health nurses and social workers have told me, 'I would never take antidepressant medication.' Why is that? There seems to be such pressure, such pride, in the fact that they would not take, or need to take, medication, as if it might show weakness.

Perhaps through having had a mental illness and recovered, a person learns to cope and is in some ways better because of it. There are many ways in which I believe I am much better off because of what has happened to me. No doubt others can vouch for that also. At this stage of my life, for instance, I am happy to spend time alone and enjoy it. There are things now which I can enjoy, unhampered by work demands, children, and other worthwhile things which belonged to the past. Having spent many hours alone in my childhood and in the many months of hospitalisation, I am no stranger to aloneness and have learned to love it, to use it and to be thankful for it. Long lonely days separated from the bonds of mankind were special; they enabled an experience, different perhaps, more intense, and painful but full of possibilities for change and growth.

And so part of writing this has been to recognise that having had a mental illness, or any adversity, can change you. People who have been dogged by stigma, have perhaps struggled to be accepted and to gain employment, or have felt sensitive about their past and unable to talk about it – all this may in fact have made a person stronger. My own life, I see as a gift. It is truly a gift, because of how it has changed me.

Life is happy for me now – simple, but very satisfying, and at last I know what a happy couple is. Peace, quiet, apart from the phone, the promise of no sudden noises, a time to cherish the journey. It has all been worthwhile. You value more what you wait for, and struggle after all is part of life, a life well lived.

**Life**

In this world of hustle and bustle
Where time is the essence of all,
It's hard to find a person
With the time to stop and to share

The most beautiful lasting memories
Are feelings and thoughts that are shared,
They last for only a moment
But are the ones that will always remain.

So is time so very important
Or the things and possessions we gain
In a lifetime that lasts but a moment
In the endless passage of time.

Though things can be taken, possessions be lost
Love lasts forever and always remains.
The love of God is certain
As His command to us for sure,
That we should 'love one another'
In the same way He loves us.

# Epilogue

She sat in her office gazing out the window at the roses. They seemed to follow her from her childhood. Grass, lawns, the smell of newly mown grass, she loved them all. It must have been the standard practice in those days to plant roses in hospitals because she always worked in hospitals and they were always there. She inhaled the warm fermented fragrance of the freshly mown lawn, it entered her being and she felt a warmth around her heart. A message of hope perhaps. And she was happy. She loved her work. But now she was ready to retire. Within her again stirred the desire to begin writing her story. Finally. She had planned to do it since she was in her twenties.

She had needed to wait a while; there were reasons why it could not be written yet. But now it was time. She spent more and more time gazing out the window of her office. She dreamed of free time to gather up her thoughts, bundle up the past and put it all together again. 'I want to write,' she thought but the voice, again the voice, interrupted her. 'Why? What for? Who is interested in your story?' it said. Years ago, the voice dumped itself into her thoughts. 'Stop now,' it would say. And she stopped.

But now she could feel the words coming fast, and images from the past as well. Whole paragraphs raced through her mind, bumping into each other, trying to jump the queue. She needed to hold them down, staple them to the page so as not to lose them.

The voice kept on and I listened to it. Time passed and I grew older. And then I had a dream.

I was going to the office of Ann O'Ryan, a social worker for whom I worked, from 1988, at Mt Henry Hospital in Perth. I heard that she was next door and I said hello. I was on my way to buy sponge cake, as the children and people around me were all eating but they wanted something more and I suggested I would go to buy a sponge cake. I did think that maybe I could have taken some of the children with me, as I had left all on my own, leaving the children for someone else to look after. I could have taken a few of them with me, but I didn't. I bought the sponge cake but found it difficult to carry with all my parcels. I had taken hours, and I was worried that I had not let the others know where I was.

I said to Ann, 'I should let them know where I am.'

'Why?' she said. 'They know where you are.'

It was pleasant chatting to Ann and her friend. It was comfortable and it felt good. Ann was trying to tidy up. There were things everywhere. She was trying to move furniture.

Then she turned to me and she said, 'I want to tell you something before you find out from someone else.'

'What is it?' I asked.

'Your name is in the paper today.'

'You're joking.'

'I'm not,' she replied.

'What? In the Sunday paper? The Sunday paper's terrible. It's almost as bad as the Sydney *Sunday Telegraph*. I never read it. It's trashy.'

'Well, your name's there.' She pointed it out. Then she went on to say, 'You know, I wasn't sure about you when I first worked with you. There was just something and I couldn't work it out but now I know.' She hugged me tight and I hugged her.

Then she showed me the article. It was like a lift-out, with lots of writing, densely printed. My name was there and it said,

> Twenty-nine people have suffered from this mental illness…

Ann could not remember any more. She showed me the paper. I looked at it. There was something written about my diagnosis. I read it.

'Well, I've been given various diagnoses, but why was I the worst psycho-neurotic patient my doctor had ever had?' I said to Ann.

The article went on to say,

'Were you not loved as a child?' and continued, 'Because this can have long lasting effects on you.'

It went on to mention many things about childhood and traumatic events.

At once I said, 'Hold on. That's my story. How did that get here? I lost the copy of my story once, the paper copy, and then I lost a second copy somewhere.'

'Where did it go? Who has it?'

We pored over it and Anne said, 'There it is. Now everyone will know. It's in the paper.'

And I said, 'Good, the world needs to know about mental illness.'

**My Day**

Today's morning bumped into me at seven
The sun warmed my bedroom walls and filtered its warmth
Placing it on my bed
Lazy long it stretched itself within me
I gazed at it and saw a pillow of happiness.

Lime green paint brushed a pathway along our curved road
A place for bikes to ride
The road wakened to motorists breathing mouths-full of tiredness
Which fell on its hard rock surface.

Wakened once more to bird calls and daily routines
They tried complaining or not at day break
Rest not for bones wearied by tomorrow's wants,
This day is for being, thus be it today

Here one finds some solace when
A quiet softness prepares
A place to be oneself inside
It founded nestled there.

www.ingramcontent.com/pod-product-compliance
Lightning Source LLC
Chambersburg PA
CBHW030911080526
44589CB00010B/248